Desserts

Desserts

Bonnie Stern

RANDOM HOUSE
Toronto

Published in 1988 in Canada by Random House of Canada Limited,
Toronto

Canadian Cataloguing in Publication Data

Stern, Bonnie
    Bonnie Stern desserts

Includes index.
ISBN 0-394-22040-4

1. Desserts.   I. Title.

TX773.S74 1988   641.8′6   C88-094476-5

DESIGN: Keith Abraham
FRONT COVER PHOTOGRAPH: Copyright © Robert Wigington
BACK COVER AUTHOR PHOTOGRAPH: Skip Dean
FOOD STYLIST: Olga Truchan
ILLUSTRATIONS: Bo-Kim Louie and David Mazierski
EDITORIAL: Shelley Tanaka

Printed and bound in Canada by T.H. Best Printing Company Limited

Contents

This book can only be dedicated to my daughter, Anna Claire.
I unconsciously named her after a dessert, and she really is so sweet.

Acknowledgments

Many calorific thanks go out to those who helped me with this book. We are all back to normal now, but everyone at the cooking school — Linda Stephen, Maureen Lollar, Marie Jones, Jennifer Naldrett, Elizabeth Renick, Julie Lewis and me — all gained a few pounds while we were testing these recipes. My husband, Ray Rupert, and his daughter Fara personally tested all the chocolate recipes, and Mark and Anna learned what every child and adult knows — chocolate chip cookie batter tastes better raw than baked.

I must also thank Shelley Tanaka, my editor, who always does much more than her job by making (she calls it testing!) the recipes that sound good to her as she is working. Robert Wigington, who photographed the shortcake for the cover, has a unique and passionate understanding of what a dessert should look like. Olga Truchan, as always, styles my recipes keeping my preferences in mind but adding her own mark of professionalism. Thanks to Bo Louie, whose illustrations are better and more instructive than any I have seen, and to Keith Abraham for his user-friendly design. At Random House, Ed Carson and Doug Pepper made this book a pleasure to work on and gave me lots of support and encouragement along the way.

There are many people who have added to my knowledge of desserts, and I've credited several of them in the recipes. No one can remember where every idea or flavor combination comes from, but if I do, I try to mention it.

I would also like to thank my students. This book is really for them (and I wouldn't go into sugar shock for just anyone!). They tell me what they need to know by asking questions and suggesting new recipes or courses. Without them, this book would not be nearly as complete or as helpful.

Introduction

There are so many reasons why I wanted to write a dessert cookbook. I began my cooking career by making desserts when I was very young, the age my children are now. I remember baking with my mother before I was five. She encouraged my love of cooking in many ways, including cleaning up after me. Even then I knew I was spoiled, and although I said I would never do the same thing for my own children, I do. And they love to bake, too.

With so many health-conscious people interested in maintaining their weight, it may seem surprising that desserts are all the rage. But there are several logical reasons for this. For one thing, we have all been eating well and exercising for so many years, we feel we deserve a little treat now and then. I also think that exercising has helped people control the quantity of food they eat — one small piece of a chocolate mousse cake can be enough. Using the best-quality ingredients may increase the price a little, but the results make the dessert worth the calories. Besides, when you need something to pick up your spirits, a delicious and elegant dessert is still less expensive than a lot of other indulgences.

Another reason desserts have become so popular is that restaurants, recognizing a growing profit center, have begun promoting desserts as they never have before — and they have been rewarded with blossoming sales. The desserts many restaurants are serving these days are almost irresistible in name alone, from homey treats like apple or pear crisps with homemade ice cream to sophisticated dishes like chocolate hazelnut dacquoise. Today, people will go to an elegant restaurant just for dessert, and many establishments are even starting to encourage this.

When you entertain at home, dessert is the last thing your guests will have at your house. Friends should leave with a sweet silky taste in their mouths and their hearts. The dessert doesn't have to be complex or rich or take a long time to make, but as long as you use the best ingredients and cook with love, you'll end every meal with a smile.

BONNIE STERN
Toronto

1

General Tips
and Techniques

M Y students often say that one of the best things about coming to my cooking classes is learning about tips that can be applied to other recipes, not just mine. Here are some hints and techniques that should help you become more successful with your dessert-making. Remember that there are many other tips, garnishing ideas and techniques in the introductions to the other chapters, and also in the individual recipes.

Equipment

Bain Marie
Custard or crustless cheesecake recipes may call for a bain marie or water bath. The dish of custard or cheesecake is placed in a larger pan filled with very hot or gently simmering water, so that the water comes halfway up the sides of the pan of custard. This technique prevents a crust from forming, prevents browning, protects the custard from too intense a heat and ensures a smooth, creamy texture.

Bakeware

Baking sheets: Jelly roll pans have a rim about 3/4 inch (2 cm) high. The most common size is 15 × 10 inches (2 L). When I need a true **cookie sheet** (a pan with a lip on one side), I turn the jelly roll pan over and use it upside down. However, cookie sheets can also be used as large spatulas for turning fish on a barbecue, transferring cakes, pies and cookies from one place to another, etc.

Cake pans: I tend to use round cake pans more than square, but I do have a 9 inch (2.5 L) square pan for bar cookies, squares and cakes. I am also fond of the old-fashioned 13 × 9 inch (3.5 L) Pyrex baking dish. I use it for crisps, cobblers and large single-layer cakes.

I like to use the deep — at least 2 inches (5 cm) — round layer cake pans. If you cannot find deep ones, sometimes a springform pan can be used instead. Remember never to fill any cake pan more than two-thirds full.

Cakes can also be made in loaf pans; the standard sizes are 8 × 4 inches (1.5 L) or 9 × 5 inches (2 L).

Pie plates and flan pans: A flan pan is actually a one-piece fluted round shallow pan with an indented bottom. You bake a sponge cake in it and, when it is inverted, it has a space for a cream filling and/or fruit. However, nowadays a flan usually refers to an open-faced fruit tart, which is made in what I call a removable-bottom quiche pan. It has two pieces, a flat bottom and a fluted edge and comes in many different sizes; the 10 inch (25 cm) pan is the most practical. After you have baked a quiche or tart in this pan, the bottom lifts out to show a freestanding crust. If the pastry base is very stable, you can slide the tart carefully onto a serving platter, but I usually just place the bottom with the tart right on the platter. You can also find lovely fluted ceramic quiche and tart pans; with these, you serve the tart right from the pan.

Although I have many fluted quiche and flan pans, I still like a plain 9 or 10 inch (23 or 25 cm) pie dish for old-fashioned desserts like lemon meringue pie and rhubarb pie.

Springform pans: A springform pan is a deep cake pan with removable sides that spring off. They come in many different sizes — 8 inch, 9 inch and 10 inch (2 L, 2.5 L and 3 L) sizes are the most common. Buy the 9 inch (2.5 L) size if you only want to have one.

Tube and Bundt pans: Tube pans are becoming easier to find again, now that angel food cake is enjoying a resurgence in popularity. I find the 10 inch (4 L) pan the most practical. Bundt is the trade name of a fluted tube pan that gives cakes an interesting shape. A ring mold ("savarin") is a shallow tube pan that is used for jelly molds or baked custards.

Bowls

It is a good idea to have an assortment of different-sized bowls both for mixing and for holding preparation ingredients (see Mise en place, page 27). You can use stainless-steel, glass, Pyrex or plastic bowls, but I prefer stainless-steel, simply because it is unbreakable.

Copper bowls are used for egg whites because there is a reaction with the copper that seems to stabilize the whites and keep them firmer longer (see page 28). However, if you add a bit of cream of tartar or lemon juice to the egg whites, the same results occur. If you do decide to invest in a copper bowl, buy one that is at least 10 inches (25 cm) across the top.

Just before they are used, copper bowls should be cleaned with a bit of salt and plain vinegar or lemon juice. I also like to use a copper bowl when I want to chill things in a hurry, as it gets very cold quickly. Just place some ice cubes and cold water in the copper bowl; set the bowl of whatever you want to chill into the ice cube/water mixture. Stir until the contents are the desired temperature.

Double Boilers

Use a double boiler when you are cooking something delicate, such as chocolate (which might burn if you used direct heat), or to avoid curdling something like a sauce made with egg yolks with no starch added. Things take longer to cook in a double boiler, but using one is a worthwhile precaution.

Double boilers can be very costly, and many have ridges up the sides of the top section, making stirring difficult. Instead of a double boiler, you can use a wide, flatish stainless-steel bowl that just sits on top of a pot and settles in only about one or two inches. Make sure the water in the bottom does not touch the bowl.

Food Mills

A food mill is one of my favorite old-fashioned gadgets. It purees and strains food at the same time. It is perfect for things like raspberries, because it removes the seeds and purees as well. Some people call it the first food processor.

If you have a food mill, you can also make applesauce or pear sauce with the peel on for more flavor and nutrients; just puree the sauce in the food mill to remove the skins. If a recipe calls for a food mill and you do not have one, simply puree the food in a blender or food processor, then press the mixture through a strainer.

Be sure to put the food mill blades in right side up — what looks like upside-down is correct!

Food Processors

A food processor is a very useful tool for baking. Just be sure not to overprocess anything. I use it often for cookies and simple cakes, but I do not usually beat egg whites in it, as it doesn't seem to beat in enough air. I use it for whipping cream when I want to thicken the cream (to resemble the texture of sour cream) but when volume is not essential (the whipped cream will not be as light, but it will be thick).

The new mini food processors are excellent for grating citrus peel and chopping nuts.

Marble Slabs

Marble slabs are used to roll out pastry because they keep the pastry cold, which should result in more tender, flaky pastry. (For bread dough or pasta, wood or a warmer surface is preferable.) They are also useful when working with chocolate, caramel and sugar, because they chill things so quickly. However, they are very heavy, so be prepared to find a permanent place on your counter for the slab, or build it in.

Just before using your marble slab, chill it by placing a jelly roll pan of ice cubes on the slab for about 10 minutes. (Be sure to wipe the slab dry before using.)

Measuring Cups and Spoons

You should have sets of graduated measures for dry ingredients like flour and sugar, in both metric and imperial, as well as glass measuring cups with imperial on one side and metric on the other. I also like the large 8 cup (2 L) batter bowls. You can make a batter in them, and if it has to be divided between two pans, you can easily see how much goes in each. Batter bowls are also great for heating and cooking sauces in the microwave.

Mixers

I like a hand mixer with round wire beaters rather than flat wires. The round wires beat more air into things and resemble a hand whisk more closely, though they are harder to find. I use hand mixers for less than 2 cups (500 mL) cream, a couple of egg whites, or mixtures that are too small for my heavy-duty mixer.

My favorite heavy-duty mixers come with three different attachments: a dough hook for yeast mixtures, a "K-beater" for creaming mixtures, and a balloon whisk made of many large round wires for beating egg whites and whipping cream.

Ovens

Convection ovens: In a convection oven, a fan circulates the air through the oven so that food bakes more evenly and a little more quickly than usual. The commercial ovens I used in my chef training were miraculous, but the home models that imitate them cannot possibly work as well.

Gas or electric ovens: I prefer gas burners and gas ovens for cooking, although some people find that the temperature control in an electric oven is more accurate. Whatever kind of oven you have, you should use a thermometer to make sure the temperature is correct (see Thermometers).

Microwave ovens: I really do love my microwave, although I have to admit I use it mainly for defrosting, reheating and all kinds of little jobs like melting chocolate and butter and toasting nuts. Because I usually cook in large quantities, or make things that are very quick to cook conventionally, microwave ovens do not help me as much as they would most people.

Parchment Paper

Parchment paper is non-stick silicone paper that is used to line baking sheets and cake pans so food doesn't stick. Sometimes I butter and flour the parchment if I want a butter taste on the outside of my finished dessert — follow the instructions in the individual recipes. I also use it to line the pastry when I bake blind (see page 83). The parchment is less likely to stick than foil or waxed paper, and because the paper is porous, the crust also bakes better.

Once you get used to using parchment paper, you will find it hard to bake without it. In some cases it can be wiped clean and reused.

Pastry Brushes

Pastry brushes are wonderful for basting, brushing on glazes and buttering pans. Be sure to wash them thoroughly.

Pastry Cloths and Rolling Pin Covers

Everyone seems to have a preferred way of rolling out pastry, but when I was starting out, the thing that helped me the most was a rolling pin cover and pastry cloth. Lay out the cloth on the counter (place a slightly damp cloth underneath to hold it in place if it slips). Place the stocking over your rolling pin (see page 82). Flour the cloth and pin lightly.

Pie Weights

When a pie crust is prebaked or baked "blind" (see page 83), weights are placed in the parchment paper-lined pie shell to hold the pastry down and prevent it from puffing during baking. You can buy aluminum or ceramic pie weights, or just use dried beans or rice. (Don't use popcorn.)

Piping Tubes

A piping tube can make the most ordinary dessert look fancy and complicated, but it is very easy to use (see page 33). I like using a cloth piping tube that is about 14 inches (34 cm) long. I use a variety of nozzles, but my favorites are a plain cone with a tip about 1/8 inch (3 mm) wide for writing, and a plain tip about 3/4 inch (2 cm) wide for ladyfingers, cream puff pastry and meringues. I also like star tips for rosettes. When you buy the bags, you usually have to trim the points a bit to fit the nozzles. Just be sure not to trim off too much. Clean the bags with soap and warm water after using and place over a bottle neck to dry.

You can also make disposable piping cones for piping different-colored icings, especially when you want a very fine line. Start with a large isosceles triangle of waxed paper or parchment paper (the long side should be at least 12 inches (30 cm). Place it on the counter with the point away from you and the long side near you. Take the two side points and rotate them until they all join at the far point (see diagram). Secure the cone by folding down the edges. Fill with icing or chocolate and fold the top over. Cut the tip to the size you wish.

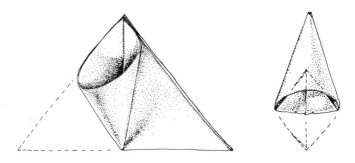

You can also put icing into a zip-lock bag and cut off one of the corners. Or you can use plastic mustard or ketchup squeeze bottles.

Pots
Heavy pots and pans make cooking easier. They will retain heat, allowing you to use a lower heat and therefore reducing the chances of burning.

Rolling Pins
There are many kinds of rolling pins, but if I could only have one, I would want a large wooden one on ball bearings, with the pin at least 12 inches (30 cm) long. This pin can be used for pastry, bread dough or pizza.

Scales
Measuring would actually be a lot easier if we weighed our ingredients, but because not everyone has a set of kitchen scales,

measurements are usually given by volume instead of by weight. (If you have a European cookbook, you will notice that everything is measured by weight.) I like to have a set of scales for weighing cream cheese and other things that you do not always buy in exact amounts, like large slabs of chocolate. Usually a scale that goes up to 2 lb (1 kg) will weigh small amounts more accurately than a scale that goes up to 10 lb (5 kg). And it will be much easier to read!

Spatulas

I like to have an assortment of plastic spatulas. None of them last indefinitely (my food processor "eats" up many!). I like the really large ones for folding egg whites, the medium-sized ones for general purposes, the long narrow ones for scraping out jars, and the new tiny ones for small jars and the mini food processors. For baking you will probably also want a long metal spatula with a slightly flexible blade for icing cakes.

Strainers

Strainers are useful for obvious straining tasks (if a sauce has lumps in it in the kitchen, there is no reason it should have lumps when it reaches the dining room). You can also use a strainer to sift flour with other ingredients, drain pasta, wash fruit and to dust icing sugar or cocoa on top of desserts. Stainless-steel strainers are ideal, but they are usually quite expensive. However, the plastic ones tear easily, and other metal strainers sometimes rust. Be sure to clean them thoroughly.

Thermometers

It is important to have a thermometer in your oven, your refrigerator and your freezer. You can buy thermometers especially for these purposes. They will tell you whether your kitchen appliances are working properly.

Candy thermometers are also useful if you make a lot of candy. They eliminate much of the guesswork.

Turntables

Although turntables are not really necessary, they will help give your cakes a truly professional look. They look like small lazy Susans.

Place your cake on a cardboard round or a serving plate lined with strips of waxed paper (see page 37). Center the cake on the turntable. Then hold a narrow spatula against the side of the cake, perpendicular to the plate and at a 30 degree angle to the cake. Turn the table with your other hand and allow it to spin. The smooth look of the icing is truly miraculous.

Whisks

There are two basic kinds of whisks. The ones that have a small loop joining all the wires at the top are mainly for beating and smoothing out sauces; the larger ones with more flexible wires are for beating egg whites and whipping cream.

Ingredients

Baking Powder

Baking powder is a leavening agent. Nearly all baking powder now is double-acting. This means it contains one acid that bubbles when combined with wet ingredients at room temperature, and another that activates at oven temperatures. (If you do not have double-acting baking powder, see page 23 for a substitute.) Buy baking powder in small quantities and keep it dry and tightly sealed. Replace it every six months. To see if your baking powder is still active, combine 1 tsp (5 mL) with 1/2 cup (125 mL) hot water. If it does not fizz frantically, it's too old to use.

Baking Soda

Baking soda is used to neutralize acid ingredients and leaven baked goods. If it is kept very dry, it should last for about one year. When you feel it is too old for baking, you can always pour it down the drain to clean out your kitchen pipes, place the opened box in the refrigerator to absorb unwanted odors, or even sprinkle it in kitty litter.

Butter

Nothing beats the taste of butter. I know it is an extravagance these days with everyone watching their weight and cholesterol intake, but my philosophy is to eat only foods that are high in calories if they taste absolutely delicious! I have cut back dramatically on the amount of butter I use, but I would rather eat one small cookie made with butter than a whole bunch made with margarine or shortening. If it doesn't taste wonderful, why eat it at all?

I usually use unsalted butter in all my baking and cooking. Unsalted butter burns less quickly, has a fresher taste and does not add unnecessary salt. If you do not use butter up fairly quickly, cut each pound into quarters — 1/2 cup (125 mL) in each piece — wrap well and freeze. When a recipe calls for creaming butter, I try to have it at room temperature because it is easier to handle that way. If I have forgotten to take it out of the refrigerator, I cut the butter into bits and warm my mixing bowl with hot water before trying to beat. If I am using a food processor, I prefer the butter cold, as the intense speed of the processor tends to warm up the ingredients.

Clarified butter is not often used in baking, since you usually want the full dairy flavor. When you clarify butter you remove the milk solids, which makes the butter less likely to burn in cooking and also enables it to be stored longer. To clarify butter, melt it and skim any froth from the surface. Cool to room temperature and refrigerate. When the butter is solid, discard the liquidy milk mixture underneath the hard yellow part at the top. Although the solid clarified butter does not, strictly speaking, have to be kept cold, I always do refrigerate it. Use it in recipes where burning and sticking can be a problem (such as crêpes or omelets).

Cheese

The cheese used in desserts should be fresh, sweet and usually mild. When **cream cheese** is called for, you can use the solid cream cheese or the creamy-style cream cheese unless the recipe specifies otherwise. When **cottage cheese** is called for, it usually refers to the solid curd cottage cheese that comes wrapped in paper and plastic, as opposed to the creamy-style curds purchased in tubs. **Ricotta** is a rich Italian cottage cheese and usually comes in tubs. Drain it before using, if there is any liquid in the bottom. Ricotta can usually replace either solid curd cottage cheese (for a slightly richer result) or cream cheese (for a slightly lighter result). **Mascarpone** is a very rich Italian cream cheese. It is used in the famous Italian dessert, tiramisu (see page 171). Although you can buy domestic mascarpone, the imported Italian variety, although slightly more expensive, is much better.

Chocolate

European chocolate is generally much smoother, less sweet and better tasting than domestic chocolate. And in some cases the price is almost the same. There are also definite differences in taste, sweetness, bitterness, acidity and texture among European chocolates, although none are too hard to eat! My favorite brands right now are Lindt from Switzerland, Callebaut from Belgium and Cacao Barry from France.

Unsweetened chocolate is used primarily in cooking. It contains the highest percentage of chocolate liquor of all the chocolates. It is approximately 50 to 58 percent cocoa butter and has no sugar.

Bittersweet chocolate contains approximately 35 percent chocolate liquor, so it has a strong chocolate taste. It also contains cocoa butter, sugar, lecithin and vanilla or vanillin. It can be used in place of semisweet or sweet chocolate.

Semisweet chocolate usually contains between 15 and 35 percent chocolate liquor. It has more sugar and less chocolate flavor than bittersweet.

Sweet chocolate is the sweetest of the sweetened chocolates. It has the least amount of chocolate liquor and the most amount of sugar.

Milk chocolate contains milk powder. It usually contains less than 15 percent chocolate liquor and therefore does not have nearly the chocolate flavor of dark chocolate. Although it is the favorite eating chocolate for many people, myself included, true chocoholics find it bland.

White chocolate does not contain any chocolate liquor, which causes the flavor to be very light. It should contain cocoa butter (not vegetable fat), milk solids, sugar and vanilla or vanillin. If you are using white chocolate, buy the very best you can find (usually imported is better than domestic), since some white chocolates have a very sweet, artificial taste.

Many professionals like to use a type of chocolate called **couverture** for cooking and chocolate-making. It contains more cocoa butter than regular bittersweet chocolate and therefore is smoother in texture and a little easier to handle. It can be used interchangeably with bittersweet chocolate.

Coating chocolate is not really a chocolate but a chocolate-flavored mixture. It is also called compound chocolate, summer coating or confectionery coating. The cocoa butter normally found in chocolate is replaced by vegetable fats. Though coating chocolate is less expensive than regular chocolate, it is normally very sweet with artificial undertones. It is very easy to use when making decorations and does not have to be tempered (see page 30), but the flavor is inferior to real chocolate. (I have recently found one coating chocolate that I like — Callebaut from Belgium — although it is hard to find and more expensive than most coating chocolates.

Cocoa powder is unsweetened chocolate with much of the cocoa butter removed. Cocoa can be Dutch-processed (processed with alkali) or "natural." Nearly all imported cocoa is Dutch-processed, making it less acidic and darker in color than regular cocoa.

Chocolate should be wrapped well and stored at room temperature in a dry, dark place. Unsweetened, bittersweet or semisweet chocolate will keep well for over a year. Milk chocolate should only be kept for nine to twelve months. I do not like to keep white chocolate longer than a few months, and chocolate that contains fruit or nuts does not keep well for longer than a month.

Coffee

When coffee is used in baking, it is usually used as a flavoring. Therefore the flavor should be more intense than the coffee you drink. Most of the time I use either espresso coffee or instant espresso powder (though it can be difficult to find). If I am using regular coffee,

I prefer brewed to instant. I make triple-strength brewed coffee for baking.

Cream

If a recipe calls for a specific type of cream, use the one indicated in the recipe. If the type of cream is not specified, you can use any type. **Crème fraîche** is a cultured cream that is high in fat and found in European countries. It combines the sweetness of heavy cream with the bite and texture of sour cream. It is very special and delicious. Sometimes you can buy it in specialty shops, but it is expensive and I usually prefer to make it (see page 187).

Eggs

I always buy extra-large eggs for cooking and baking. Generally speaking, you can use large or extra-large eggs in the recipes in this book. Brown eggs and white eggs have the same nutritive value, but I find there are more blood spots and brown specks in brown eggs.

Eggs should be kept in their original packaging or in a covered container in the refrigerator, not on an open egg shelf, since egg shells are porous and can absorb flavors from other foods. Eggs will spoil quickly at room temperature. If you find a cracked egg in your package, discard it. If you crack an egg accidentally yourself, use it quickly.

To determine how fresh an egg is, break one onto a plate. A fresh egg will have a high yolk, and the white will be close around the yolk.

Egg whites freeze well. Freeze them individually in ice cube trays and then transfer to a sturdy plastic bag, or freeze several of them in a container; there are approximately four egg whites in 1/2 cup (125 mL). Egg yolks do not freeze as successfully.

Flour

Use the type of flour specified in each recipe. Although there are ways to substitute one flour for another if necessary (see page 24), the texture of the finished product is rarely the same. For information about measuring flour, see page 27. For information about sifting flour, see page 29.

Lemons

I always like to have fresh lemons on hand. When you need a quick garnish, lemons can brighten a plate in seconds; when a sauce needs a pick-me-up, often lemon juice does the trick. Grated lemon peel gives an intense zesty taste to food, and I cannot think of a flavor that is more refreshing. Even after a heavy meal, a rich but lemony mousse or ice cream seems light.

If you need lemon peel, grate it before trying to juice the lemon.

Lemon peel can be grated with a zester or with the finest side of a four-sided grater, or it can be removed with a vegetable peeler or knife, and then chopped. My favorite new kitchen gadget is the new mini food processor. It does a fabulous job of "grating" lemon peel, which cannot be equaled by the larger machines.

Grated lemon peel can be frozen. Spread the peel on a baking sheet and freeze. Then place in plastic bags; the peel will stay granular. Use it straight from the freezer. You will get 1 to 2 tsp (5 to 10 mL) grated peel from one lemon.

To get more juice out of a lemon, roll it on the counter first. This softens the lemon and allows juice to flow more freely. Then cut the lemon in half and squeeze the juice between your fingers (see also *Limes*). Extra fresh lemon juice can be frozen in ice cube trays (be sure to label them) for easy measuring and defrosting — one ice cube equals 2 tbsp (25 mL) juice.

Limes

The frustrating thing about limes is that often you can hardly get any juice out of them (and they are usually too hard to soften by rolling them on the counter)! Here's a terrific tip. If you need the peel, grate that first. Then heat the lime using any of the following methods. If you have a microwave, poke a few holes in the limes and place them in a glass measure. Microwave at High (100%) for about 20 seconds per lime. Do not squeeze them until you are sure they are cool. If you do not have a microwave, place the pierced limes in an ovenproof dish and bake at 350° F (180° C) for 5 minutes. Or, do not pierce the limes and place them in boiling water for one minute. This trick also works for hard lemons.

Oranges

Treat orange peel the same as lemon peel. I usually use freshly squeezed orange juice or, if I want an intense orange flavor but not too much liquid, I often use frozen orange juice concentrate.

Nuts

Although it is often less expensive to buy nuts in bulk food stores, make sure the nuts are fresh. Nuts generally are high in fat, and this fat can turn rancid. Walnuts are notorious for going off quickly. If you are buying more nuts than you are likely to use within a week or two, store them in the freezer.

I like to toast nuts before using them, as it greatly intensifies their flavor. Place the nuts on a baking sheet and bake at 350° F (180° C) for 5 to 10 minutes. Chop or grind the nuts after toasting. (I prefer to buy whole nuts and chop or grind them myself, as they lose flavor more quickly after they have been processed.)

Ground nuts are sometimes used as flour in cakes or tortes. They must be ground carefully, or the essential oils will be released and they will become pasty. Ground nuts should be very fine but not moist.

Nuts can be ground by being chopped over and over again (as in a food processor), but I like to use an old-fashioned "mouli" grinder. It requires a little patience, but the nuts will be light and free-flowing. The grinder works well because the nuts only go through it once, whereas in a food processor they are chopped over and over again. If you are using a food processor, grind no more than 1 cup (250 mL) at a time. If you can, add some of the sugar from the recipe to help keep them light. Process on and off, watching closely. The new mini food processors do a better job on nuts, but you can only grind about 1/3 cup (75 mL) at a time.

If you overprocess nuts and end up with a paste, simply add some sugar and liqueur, shape into balls, roll in melted chocolate and call them nut truffles!

Finely chopped nuts should be in tiny pieces, not ground. Use a large chef's knife with a triangular blade. Place the nuts in the center of your work surface and chop back and forth, gently holding the tip of your knife down. If you are chopping nuts in a food processor, watch them closely and use on/off pulses.

Coarsely chopped nuts should be in chunky pieces. **Whole nuts** or halves are usually used for garnishing.

Almonds keep well and have a wonderful flavor, especially when toasted. I usually buy and use them with their skins on, as I feel it increases the flavor, fiber and gives an interesting color to desserts and cookies. But every once in a while you need to remove the skins. You can buy blanched almonds, or you can blanch them yourself. Place the nuts in boiling water for 5 minutes. Chill in cold water. The skins should just slip off.

Hazelnuts are sometimes called filberts. Actually they are slightly different, but can be used interchangeably. They are usually sold shelled but whole. I like to remove a little of their papery skins before using them. After toasting the hazelnuts, while they are warm, rub them, in batches, between tea towels to remove the skins (don't worry if you can't get all the skins off). Another method that sometimes works well is to put the toasted nuts into the food processor with the plastic blade. They fly around the machine furiously and most of the skins come off. Hazelnuts and almonds are interchangeable in most recipes; both keep well.

I often use **pecans** if I cannot find good walnuts. They keep a little better than walnuts and are now widely available.

Pine nuts have become very popular lately, with the increased interest in Mediterranean, Southwestern and oriental cooking. They freeze well. They are used in pesto sauce, and therefore are usually easy to find in Italian delicatessens or even Middle Eastern shops, if your local nut supplier cannot help you.

Most people eat **pistachio nuts**, but I prefer to cook with them. Many nut shops, bulk food stores and Middle Eastern stores sell pistachio nuts already shelled, which is a great boon to the cook. They should be salt- and sugar-free. If you are buying them in their shells, look for unsalted natural-colored ones.

When **walnuts** are fresh, they are very delicious, but it seems to be getting harder to find good ones. I often buy prepackaged walnuts because they have a high turnover and there seems to be a better chance of them staying fresh. Always taste walnuts before using; if they are bitter or rancid, do not use them.

Salt

I do not use much salt in desserts. If you find any of the desserts "bland," you can add a pinch of salt, but please use discretion. I always use unsalted butter, so if you do like salt, you may miss it. However, I find that once you get used to not using salt, other flavors come through much more clearly.

Vanilla and Other Extracts

I use only pure vanilla extract as the artificial one, I find, leaves a strange aftertaste. Even though pure vanilla is becoming quite costly, I think it is worth the price. Vanilla beans can be used to flavor sauces and custards. The best beans are pliable and very fragrant. If you want a gentle flavor, cut the beans into pieces before using. Once used, do not throw them away. Rinse and dry. Store them in the bottom of your sugar canister. They will flavor your sugar, and you will need less vanilla extract in the recipes you use the sugar in. The beans can be reused a few times. If you want a very strong vanilla flavor, slit the pods and scrape the seeds into the sauce. (You can store the pods in your sugar canister.)

I also use pure almond extract. For other flavorings, see the liqueur section or notes on coffee.

Substitutions

Always take substitutions with a grain of salt; sometimes they work better than at other times. Here are the main substitutions for dessert-making. Use them with common sense and the realization that most of the time it is better to substitute than to leave an ingredient out. For liqueur substitutes, see page 25.

In addition to the following substitutions, when a dessert easily lends itself to being prepared in a lighter fashion, I have mentioned this at the end of the recipe. Although I do not like to use so-called "diet" products, I understand that people may want to reduce the fat in their diets but still eat delicious desserts. Many of the desserts in this book are not high in calories or fat, but some of the ones that are can be made lighter. Keep in mind that the result will never be the same, but it may still be very good (and you may even prefer it).

Baking Powder
For 1 tsp (5 mL) baking powder, use 1/2 tsp (2 mL) cream of tartar and 1/4 tsp (1 mL) baking soda.

Butter
You can substitute "firm" margarine or shortening for butter in most recipes. If butter is a main ingredient used for flavor, however, as in shortbread cookies or pound cake, using a substitute may change the taste considerably.

Buttermilk
In most recipes you can use sour cream or unflavored yogurt in place of buttermilk or vice versa. If you are making a dough, however, you may need another tablespoon or two of sour cream or yogurt to moisten it. You can also make a sour milk mixture by placing 1 tbsp (15 mL) plain vinegar or lemon juice in a 1 cup (250 mL) measure and filling it up with milk. Allow to rest for 5 minutes before using. Use in place of 1 cup (250 mL) buttermilk, sour cream or yogurt.

Cheese
If a recipe calls for cream cheese, you can usually use well-drained pressed solid curd cottage cheese that has been smoothed out in a food processor or blender, or ricotta cheese.

Chocolate
If you are out of unsweetened chocolate, use 3 tbsp (50 mL) cocoa plus 1 tbsp (15 mL) butter for every ounce (30 g) chocolate. Generally I don't like to substitute cocoa for sweetened chocolate, but if you are desperate, try 1-1/2 tbsp (20 mL) cocoa, 1 tbsp (15 mL) granulated

sugar and 2 tsp (10 mL) butter for every ounce (30 g) unsweetened chocolate.

Bittersweet, semisweet and sweet chocolate are interchangeable, although I prefer to use bittersweet (see page 17).

When measuring chocolate, 3 oz (90 g) chocolate equals about 1/2 cup (125 mL) chopped.

Coffee

For 1/2 cup (125 mL) extra-strong brewed coffee, use 2 tsp (10 mL) instant coffee dissolved in 1/2 cup (125 mL) hot water.

Cream

Whipping cream, heavy cream, clotted cream and crème fraîche are usually interchangeable, since they all have a fat content of over 30 percent. These creams will all whip. If you need light cream, dilute these creams by half with milk. You can usually substitute whipping cream for lighter creams, but you cannot always use a lighter cream for whipping cream. Light cream won't whip, and sometimes sauces may not thicken.

If a recipe calls for whipping cream in baking, use 3/4 cup (175 mL) milk plus 1/3 cup (75 mL) butter for every cup (250 mL) whipping cream.

Flour

For 1 cup (250 mL) all-purpose flour use 1 cup (250 mL) plus 2 tbsp (25 mL) cake and pastry flour; use 7/8 cup (200 mL) all-purpose whole wheat flour. Using whole wheat flour in place of white flour in desserts usually results in a heavier texture. I usually try using half whole wheat and half white the first time to judge if I can substitute completely.

If a recipe calls for 1 cup (250 mL) "self-raising flour," use 1 cup (250 mL) all-purpose flour plus 1 tsp (5 mL) baking powder. If you wish, add a pinch of salt.

Lemon Juice

The juice of one lemon equals 2 to 3 tbsp (25 to 50 mL). The grated peel of one lemon equals 1 to 2 tsp (5 to 10 mL). Lemon, lime and orange peel can be used interchangeably. When I use orange juice in place of lemon or lime juice, I often use frozen concentrate for a stronger orange flavor.

Nuts

If you are allergic to nuts, as long as they are not acting as the "flour" in a recipe (as in a nut torte), they can usually be omitted. Sometimes you can substitute raisins or other chopped dried fruits in their place, or chopped sweet chocolate. Or try using dry roasted chickpeas for a low-fat crunchy nut substitute.

Sugar

One cup (250 mL) granulated sugar can be replaced by 1 cup (250 mL) packed brown sugar, 2 cups (500 mL) sifted icing sugar, or 1-1/4 cups (300 mL) fruit sugar. If you want to use honey (7/8 cup/200 mL), molasses (1-1/4 cups/300 mL) or corn syrup (1 cup/250 mL), you must reduce the liquid in the recipe or increase the flour by 1/4 cup (50 mL).

In most recipes it is possible to reduce the amount of sugar by one-quarter without affecting quality. However, my recipes are usually a little less sweet than most — try them the way I have written them first to see if they suit you.

Vanilla

Use half the amount of pure almond extract; however, the flavor will be different.

Cooking with Wine and Liqueurs

If you bought every liqueur that was called for in cookbooks and food magazines, not only would it cost a fortune, but you might have to build a special cupboard just to store it all!

You can, however, easily get away with just a few liqueurs, and if you cannot or don't want to use alcohol in your cooking, there are some good substitutes.

If I could only have three liqueurs for cooking, I would want dark rum, an orange liqueur and a reasonably priced Cognac. Dark rum has more flavor than white rum, and even though I am not a rum drinker, I do like to use it in cooking. You can usually use it in place of other liqueurs. But remember that it is not sweet. Therefore when I am substituting it for a sweet liqueur, I may add a little extra sugar to the recipe.

Specialty liqueurs can come and go in fashion, but orange liqueur is always popular. It can be used in place of any fruit liqueur and seems to go well with anything from chocolate to fruit salads. Expensive orange liqueurs like Grand Marnier and Cointreau are fantastic, but less-expensive domestic brands usually work well in cooking.

Cognac is an acquired taste, but once acquired, it is hard to beat. It is perfect for flambés and is also good in chocolate desserts and cakes. Cognac is smoother than brandy and, although there is a significant price difference, I like to cook with a VS Cognac if I can.

Cognac or brandy are also good substitutes for Scotch, Bourbon or rye.

In addition to those three "staple" liqueurs, I love either Chambord or Framboise raspberry liqueur (the first is sweet; the second reminds me of fire water but has a wonderful flavor), especially in anything chocolate. And although Amaretto has been greatly overused, I still like it in apricot desserts or anything nutty. A coffee liqueur like Kahlua is great to have, too, although I do not use it that often.

If you do not want to use liqueurs, there are many other natural substitutes. Extra-strong coffee can be substituted for rum, coffee liqueur, and anywhere else you think the flavor will go well. Frozen orange juice concentrate is a great substitute for orange liqueur and other fruit liqueurs. Frozen raspberry concentrate is also a good strong fruit substitute for a liqueur. Grated orange peel can give the impression that an alcoholic product has been used. In some cases I may use a small amount of pure vanilla extract or pure almond extract as a substitute for a liqueur.

Wines used in desserts, such as port, sherry, Marsala and Madeira, can often be substituted for one another. When a recipe calls for a wine, always use the driest product available unless otherwise specified. Fruit juices can often be used in place of wines. Sometimes ginger ale makes a good substitute in fruit salads, or even just sparkling mineral water. However, remember that there are no exact substitutes, and that the demands of each recipe are usually slightly different. So experiment gently!

Flambés

Flambés are done for three reasons. The first is to burn off the alcohol. If the alcohol is not burned off, there is sometimes a slightly bitter undertaste in the finished dish. In addition, when the alcohol disappears so do many of the calories and, of course, no one can get drunk from their food. (If a sauce containing alcohol is brought to the boil, the alcohol will also evaporate.) The second reason for flambé-ing is to singe the top of a dish. Crêpe edges will darken slightly and resemble the look of being run under a hot salamander (professional gas broiler). If you do not want to flambé, you can also just place the dish under a preheated broiler. Watch it closely, though.

The third reason for flambéing is for the show. And it is pretty showy.

Whenever you are flambéing, here are a few tips:
• If you have long hair, pull it back from the sides of your face.
• Have all the equipment and ingredients you need nearby. Some people like to use long fireplace matches, which solve the problem of having to light the match at the exact moment the alcohol begins to evaporate.

• If you have a smoke detector, turn it off before flambéing, or you may end up with more company than you expected!

• The alcohol must be hot before it will ignite. You can place the amount of liquor you need in a small saucepan and heat it. Then ignite it and carefully pour it, flaming, over the food. Be sure to start at the edge of the food farthest from you. Otherwise you will find your arm in the flame.

• The other way to flambé is to pour the liquor over the food, heat it, and then ignite it as the alcohol starts to evaporate. Pour the amount of liquor you need into a glass, rather than pouring from the bottle. That way you cannot accidentally add too much or ignite the alcohol in the bottle.

• Wait for the flames to die down before serving the dish.

• Do not use too much liquor. Not only will it burn too much, but it can also make a dish taste too "boozy."

Mise en Place

Every cook has had the experience of placing a dessert in the oven, turning around and seeing one of the ingredients on the counter instead of in the dessert! The most important thing I learned in my chef training was to be organized and always have a mise en place! Before beginning to cook, *read through the whole recipe.* Then assemble all the ingredients on the counter. As you use them, transfer them to another location. Then all it takes is a glance to see if everything has been included.

If you are cooking more than one dish, read through all the recipes and double up on tasks. This can save a lot of time if there are apples to be peeled, butter to be melted, etc., in more than one recipe.

Measuring

When I cook, I generally do not worry about measuring too accurately, except when I am testing recipes. If you understand cooking and cook a great deal, you somehow know how much of everything to put into things. When I bake, however, I am much more precise.

If you are measuring flour, dip your exact measure into your canister to overflowing. Do not shake it down. Instead, level it off with the flat side of a knife. Sugar or other dry ingredients that are denser than flour usually find their own level, but if not, even them off as well. When you are measuring wet ingredients, use glass measuring cups and gauge the measure at eye level.

You should follow a recipe either in metric or imperial; try not to combine both.

Dessert Techniques

Here are some general techniques that you'll use in all kinds of recipes. For more specific techniques, see the introductions to the appropriate chapters, or the index.

Separating Eggs

When you separate eggs, you want to end up with the whites in one bowl and the yolks in another. You must do this carefully, as egg whites do not whip well if there is even the tiniest bit of the fatty egg yolk in them.

The safest way to separate eggs is with three bowls in front of you — one small one and two medium ones. The medium ones are for the accumulated egg yolks and whites; the smaller bowl is for the new white you get from each cracked egg. That way if one egg yolk breaks into one white, you haven't "contaminated" all the whites.

Eggs separate best when they are cold. Crack the side of the egg gently on the counter. Pull it gently apart with your thumbs on the bottom and your forefingers on the top. Allow the egg white to drain out of the small crack into the bowl, then break the egg shell apart so that the yolk is resting in one half. Pour the yolk from one shell to the other, allowing any excess white to drain into the rest of the white. Be careful not to break the yolk. If the second half of the shell is too small or crumbles, strain through your fingers. (Some chefs even prefer to separate eggs through their fingers, but I prefer to use the egg shells.)

Beating Egg Whites

Although books often recommend beating egg whites when they are at room temperature, I usually beat them when they are cold, since I always forget to remove them from the refrigerator in time. And I have never been dramatically disappointed with my results. But you must make sure there is not even one little bit of egg yolk in the whites; the yolk contains fat, which will inhibit the whites from beating properly. Also make sure that the bowl and beaters are perfectly clean. (If you are using a copper bowl, treat it as outlined on page 11.)

If I am not using a copper bowl, I usually add about 1/4 tsp (1 mL) cream of tartar or 1/2 tsp (2 mL) lemon juice for every four egg whites. This makes the whites a little more stable after they have been beaten. You can use a large wire whisk, hand mixer or heavy-duty mixer for beating egg whites. Stir in the cream of tartar or lemon juice at the start and slowly begin just to loosen the whites. Beat faster until the whites are frothy and just beginning to mound. If there is sugar to be added, begin now and add it slowly, a tablespoon at a time. If there isn't any sugar in the recipe, be a little more careful, as the whites tend to become overbeaten more easily. When egg whites are overbeaten, they appear dry and seem to break apart when stirred instead of being creamy and smooth.

There are many ways to see if the egg whites are ready. If a peak of egg white keeps its shape and doesn't fall over, the whites are usually firm enough, but I usually just turn the bowl upside down (*very* carefully!). If the whites slip out as I am turning, they are not beaten enough. Many chefs finish egg whites by hand with a whisk, even if they have used a mixer to start, since it is easier to tell when to stop when you are beating by hand.

Egg whites must be used immediately after they are beaten, otherwise they deflate.

Folding

When egg whites or whipping cream have been perfectly beaten, you must fold them into the base mixture correctly in order to save all the air you so meticulously beat in. Usually the base is much denser than the fluffy egg whites, or whipped cream, so first lighten the base. Gently stir about one-quarter the amount of whites or cream into the base. Then spoon the rest of the whites or cream over the base. With a large spatula, cut through the center of the mixtures and bring the spatula toward you, gently scraping the bottom and side of the bowl as you draw it through. With your other hand, turn the bowl a quarter turn to the right. Continue to do this 8 to 10 times, which should pretty well complete the folding. Most of the time you do not worry about having a few streaks of egg whites or whipping cream left in the mixture — the important thing is not to overfold. After folding the two ingredients gently together, transfer the airy mixture carefully into the prepared pan. If you "dump" the mixture into the pan, you are sure to deflate it!

Sifting

Although most flour comes presifted, there are general rules I use when deciding whether or not to sift.

• If a recipe calls for "1 cup flour, sifted," sift it after measuring. If a recipe calls for "1 cup sifted flour," sift it before measuring.

• If a recipe calls for "flour, sifted," and I am using presifted packaged flour, I would not bother sifting unless I am mixing other ingredients with the flour. (A better way to mix dry ingredients together evenly is with a food processor. Do this in a dry, empty work bowl, with the steel knife.)

• I usually sift dry ingredients if they contain things that tend to lump together, such as baking soda, baking powder, cocoa, icing sugar and cake and pastry flour.

Melting Chocolate

Chocolate is an ingredient that demands respect. Here are some tips on how to handle it properly.

• Chocolate melts at a very low temperature. Remember that it melts in your mouth!

• Always melt chocolate over indirect heat. If you use a double boiler, make sure the water underneath is just simmering. If you use a microwave, use Medium (50%) power. Remember that when you melt chocolate, especially in the microwave, the starting temperature of the chocolate, the amount of chocolate, the size of the pieces and the dish you use will all affect the melting time. You can also place the chocolate in an ovenproof bowl in a 350° F (180° C) oven, but watch it closely.

• Remove chocolate from the source of heat before it is completely melted (still slightly holding its shape). Stir to complete the melting.

• Be sure there is not even one drop of liquid in the pot, on the spoon, etc., when melting chocolate. The chocolate could "seize" or harden up. If this happens, add a few drops of vegetable oil to smooth it out again. (Do not use butter in this case, as butter contains liquid.)

• A "bloom," or discoloration on chocolate can be caused by sugar crystals forming or cocoa butter rising to the surface, forming grayish streaks or spots. This happens because the chocolate is stored at too high a temperature or under too moist conditions. When the chocolate is melted, it will be fine.

• Professional candy-makers often "temper" chocolate — a method of redistributing the cocoa butter fats so the chocolate sets up quickly and has a high gloss. Tempering requires the chocolate to be melted and cooled to very specific temperatures, and it is easier to do in large quantities. It can be a complicated business for the home cook. Instead of tempering chocolate, I usually use good-quality imported chocolate; the flavor will be good, even though the appearance may not be absolutely perfect. If I am dipping truffles into untempered melted chocolate, I roll them in ground nuts, cocoa, icing sugar or finely chopped chocolate, which will cover any streaks. You can, of course, use coating chocolate, but the flavor is rarely as good.

Decorating Tips

There are many decorating tips in the individual recipes, but here are some ideas that you can use for your own desserts or alternate with the garnishes suggested in this book.

2

Cakes

I'VE been making cakes since I was four years old, so I was surprised to learn that so many people are intimidated by them. Cakes really are easy — all you need is confidence.

I remember taking a cake to a school party when I was ten. I had designed and decorated the cake myself; it was big and green. (Green was my favorite color.) The cake sank a little (or maybe it was a lot) in the center. My mother had just returned from Mexico and had brought back many souvenirs so, not to be deterred, I placed a "lovely" straw donkey in the center of my masterpiece. Remembering all of this, I am not surprised I actually made this weird cake, but I marvel that my mother let me out of the house with it! But my mother really is that wonderful. Now I let my own children decorate their cakes as they wish. Turquoise, purple, blue — nothing offends me. When they grow up, I hope all those colors will be out of their systems, and beautiful cakes will be the most appealing ones (until they bake with their own children, that is!).

The cakes in this chapter are special. Some are rich, moist, one-layer chocolate cakes that are truly easy to make (these cakes really are supposed to fall in the center) and even easier to eat. Some are more like cake desserts assembled with mousse mixtures or sauces. Even the more traditional cakes are so good that they are worth the effort. Read the recipes through carefully and follow them. Throwing a little of this and little of that into a cake is much more precarious than doing the same thing with a stew! If you try a cake and are disappointed, go through the recipe ingredient by ingredient, step by step. If you are absolutely convinced that you did everything right (and your oven is working properly), maybe that cake just isn't for you. Everyone has different expectations, and sometimes they just aren't the same as those of the recipe author!

Cake Tips

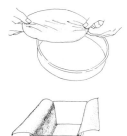

- Protect yourself from having trouble removing your cake from the pan. I like to line cake pans with parchment paper (see page 13). If I am making a round cake, I cut a circle of paper to fit the bottom only. That's because I can always run a knife around the edge of the pan to free the sides. If I am making a square, rectangular or loaf cake, I usually run the paper across the bottom and allow it to hang over two opposite sides. I can run a knife around the two other sides to free the cake, but the overhanging paper allows me to pull at it a little to help free it. I usually grease the pans first just to hold the paper in place. Otherwise it sometimes lifts up or crumples as the batter goes in.

- If a cake is baked in a Bundt-style pan, butter it with unsalted butter (it is less likely to stick or burn) and then dust it with ground nuts, breadcrumbs or, if you have nothing else, flour. Although many books call for flouring pans, I feel that the flour sometimes leaves an unpleasant film on the outside of the cake. For some cakes, like angel food, you do not have to butter or line the pan at all.

- When making cakes that have a very low (or no) flour content, do not worry if they do not rise too much, fall after rising, or even sink in the center. Usually they are very rich single-layer cakes that will taste delicious no matter what. If a cake sinks, you can level it off when it is cold. Or simply make a little more glaze and fill in the center. Another trick is to push down the sides a little once the cake has cooled.

- The most common way of telling when a cake is ready is to insert a wooden skewer, cake tester or toothpick. When it comes out dry, the cake is supposed to be ready. But this trick only works for certain cakes. With moist, dense, flourless cakes, fruit cakes or coffee cakes with sugar and cinnamon fillings, the toothpick will never come out dry.

- Another trick is to lightly touch the center of the cake when you think it should be ready. The cake should spring back to your touch. However, very moist cakes with little or no flour (e.g.

cheesecakes) should still be slightly moist in the center; the cakes firm up on cooling.

• Another common method is to wait for the cake to pull away from the sides of the pan. I don't usually depend on this one, because I think most cakes are really ready before this stage; cakes taken this far are often dry. Use a combination of all three tips, depending on the cake.

• If a cake is underbaked, you can toast individual pieces to dry it out a little; add a custard sauce and make it into a "pudding" cake; or put fruit on top and eat it as a "dessert" rather than an "official" cake. If the cake is too dry, you can soak a liqueur or sugar syrup into it; make it into a trifle by soaking it with fruit juice and adding a custard; or you can toast and butter some types of coffee cake. Be sure to note on your recipe the difference in baking time, so that the next time you make the cake, it will be better.

• When making a cake for the first time, set your timer for one-quarter to one-eighth less time than the recipe suggests and check the cake when the timer rings. This ensures that if your oven is hotter than most ovens, or your pan is wider than the one called for, the cake will still be okay.

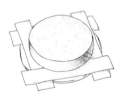

• Use waxed paper strips under the cake when you are icing it; they are removed after decorating so that the cake sits on a clean plate. Take four 10 x 2 inch (25 x 5 cm) strips of paper and arrange them along the edges of the cake while it is still in the pan (or after turning the cake out onto a rack, if you are going to ice the top instead of the bottom). Place a small circle of icing or butter in the center of the cake platter. Turn the platter upside down on top of the cake, centering it properly. Then turn the whole thing over. When the cake is cool, ice or glaze it. Remove the strips gently before the icing sets. If you are using a doily (they are gorgeous, though they often shred when you cut the cake), place it between the waxed paper and the plate.

• Professional cake decorators often crumb-coat a cake before icing to ensure that loose cake crumbs do not get into the icing. Simply spread a very thin layer of thin apricot jam, or a thin layer of icing or glaze, over the top and sides of the cake. Allow to set for a few minutes and then proceed as usual.

• Most layer and coffee cakes should be turned out of the pan after being cooled on a rack for 10 minutes, to allow air to circulate and prevent the bottom from being soggy. If the cake is turned out before this, it could fall apart (bandage it with icing or make it into a trifle); if left longer, it could stick to the pan (return it to a hot oven for 2 minutes and then turn it out).

Eggnog Roulade

YIELD: Serves 8
to 12

I developed this cake for a Christmas appearance on Dini Petty's "Cityline." It is a fabulous dessert, remarkably light and a wonderful way to end a holiday meal. Students are always afraid the cake won't really roll up. But don't worry; it will. Do not be concerned if it cracks slightly, since the whole thing is iced, anyway.

I usually serve this on a black or dark-colored tray and decorate it with some pretty holiday ornaments.

1 cup	cake and pastry flour	250 mL
1/4 tsp	baking powder	1 mL
1/2 tsp	ground nutmeg	2 mL
3	eggs, separated	3
1/3 cup	ice water	75 mL
1 cup	granulated sugar, divided	250 mL
1/2 tsp	pure vanilla extract	2 mL
	Syrup	
1/4 cup	granulated sugar	50 mL
2 tbsp	water	25 mL
1/4 cup	unsalted butter	50 mL
2 tbsp	dark rum	25 mL
2 tbsp	brandy	25 mL
	Filling and Frosting	
1-1/2 cups	whipping cream	375 mL
2 tbsp	granulated sugar	25 mL
2 tbsp	dark rum	25 mL
1 tbsp	brandy	15 mL
1 tsp	ground nutmeg	5 mL

1. Preheat oven to 325° F (160° C). Butter a jelly roll pan and line with parchment paper. Butter paper and flour lightly.

2. Sift flour with baking powder and nutmeg. Reserve.

3. In large bowl, whip egg yolks. Beat in ice water. Beat until mixture is very frothy. Add 3/4 cup (175 mL) sugar and beat until very thick and creamy, about 5 minutes. Stir in vanilla and fold in flour mixture.

4. In separate bowl, beat egg whites until light. Gradually add remaining sugar. When whites are firm, fold into yolk mixture. Spread evenly over pan.

5. Bake for 25 minutes, or until cake springs back when touched gently in center and begins to come away from sides of pan. Cool.

6. While cake is baking, prepare syrup. Combine 1/4 cup (50 mL) sugar with water and butter in a small saucepan. Bring to a boil and cook for 3 minutes. Stir in rum and brandy. Cool.

7. Dust top of cake with icing sugar and invert onto a clean tea towel. Remove pan and paper. Trim (and eat) edges of cake. Brush syrup over cake.

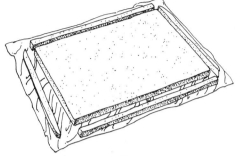

8. Whip cream until light. Add 2 tbsp (25 mL) sugar, liqueurs and nutmeg. Beat until stiff. Spread two-thirds of cream over cake. Using tea towel as a guide, roll up cake lengthwise. Carefully transfer to a long serving platter. Spread remaining cream over cake.

9. With a fork, make zigzag markings along length of cake. Grate a little additional nutmeg over cake. Garnish with holly.

A Lighter Side: Make half the amount of filling, and fill and frost the cake sparingly. It won't be quite as luscious, but it will still be delicious. (Just don't have two pieces!)

Raspberry Mirror Cake

YIELD: Serves 10 to 12

THIS is one of my very favorite cakes. The raspberry mousse can be used on its own or to fill chocolate cups. The cake can also be made without the "mirror" topping and served plain or with some whipped cream. There are lots of possibilities. If you are going to the trouble to make this cake, be sure to invest in some Chambord (raspberry liqueur). It really is wonderful, and you can buy it in tiny bottles. Fresh or individually quick frozen berries work best.

	Cake	
4	eggs, separated	4
1/2 cup	granulated sugar, divided	125 mL
1 tsp	pure vanilla extract	5 mL
2/3 cup	all-purpose flour	150 mL
	Raspberry Syrup	
1/3 cup	water	75 mL
1/3 cup	granulated sugar	75 mL
3 tbsp	raspberry liqueur	50 mL
1/2 tsp	pure vanilla extract	2 mL
	Raspberry Mousse	
2	envelopes unflavored gelatin	2
1/3 cup	water	75 mL
3	10 oz (300 g) packages frozen raspberries, or 4 cups (1 L) fresh raspberries	3
1 cup	granulated sugar	250 mL
2 tbsp	lemon juice	25 mL
3 tbsp	raspberry liqueur	50 mL
3 cups	whipping cream	750 mL
	Mirror Glaze	
1	envelope unflavored gelatin	1
3 tbsp	raspberry juice	50 mL
1/2 cup	raspberry puree (reserved from above)	125 mL
1/3 cup	red currant or raspberry jelly	75 mL
2 tbsp	raspberry liqueur	25 mL

1. Preheat oven to 350° F (180° C). Butter a 9 or 10 inch (23 or 25 cm) springform pan.

2. To make the cake, in large bowl, beat egg yolks with 1/4 cup (50 mL) sugar until very light. Beat in vanilla.

3. In separate bowl, beat egg whites until light. Slowly beat in remaining sugar. Fold whites into yolks. Sift flour over top and fold in carefully.

4. Pour batter into prepared pan and bake for 30 to 35 minutes, or until top springs back when lightly touched.

5. Meanwhile, prepare syrup. In small saucepan, cook water and sugar together until sugar dissolves, about 1 minute. Stir in liqueur and vanilla. Cool and reserve.

6. For the mousse, in small saucepan, sprinkle the gelatin over the water and allow to rest for 5 minutes to soften. Heat gelatin gently until dissolved.

7. Meanwhile, puree berries in a food mill (which purees and removes the seeds) and reserve 1/2 cup (125 mL) for glaze. You should have approximately 2 cups (500 mL) puree remaining for the mousse.

8. In saucepan, cook 2 cups (500 mL) puree with 1 cup (250 mL) sugar and lemon juice until sugar dissolves, about 5 minutes. Add liqueur.

9. Stir gelatin into raspberry mixture. Chill over a larger bowl of ice and water.

10. In bowl, beat cream until light. When raspberry mixture is cool, fold in cream.

11. To assemble, cut cool cake into three or four thin layers. Only use two layers for this recipe. (Freeze remaining layers.) Sprinkle cut side of two layers with the syrup.

12. Place one layer in bottom of a 10 inch (25 cm) springform pan. Pour in half the mousse. Top with second layer of cake. Pour in enough remaining mousse to come almost to the top of the pan. Level the mousse as perfectly as possible. Refrigerate until firm. (If there is any leftover mousse, eat it.)

13. For the mirror glaze, sprinkle gelatin over raspberry juice in small saucepan. Let soften for 5 minutes. Heat gently until dissolved.

14. In small saucepan, combine reserved raspberry puree with jelly and liqueur (heat until smooth if necessary). Stir in dissolved gelatin. Cool. Pour over mousse and swirl cake gently to level as evenly as possible. Refrigerate for at least 2 hours.

15. To serve, run a knife around inside edge of pan and free the sides. Decorate with fresh berries or edible flowers if desired, but it is gorgeous just as it is.

Praline Chocolate Dacquoise

YIELD: Serves 10
to 14

*E*VERYONE *I have ever served this to has swooned. It is worth every minute it takes to make it. In fact, it is so wonderful, I have even tripled the recipe (leaving the meringue layers in one piece) and made it as a wedding cake, decorating it with candied roses and chocolate leaves.*

This cake isn't hard to make, but it is time-consuming (the crème fraîche must be made two days ahead of time if you cannot buy it). But it freezes well, so you could make it a few weeks ahead. (I would ice it after defrosting.)

	Meringue	
6	egg whites	6
1/4 tsp	cream of tartar	1 mL
1 cup	fruit sugar	250 mL
1/2 cup	ground toasted almonds	125 mL
1/2 cup	ground toasted hazelnuts	125 mL
1 tbsp	cornstarch	15 mL
	Praline Filling	
1-1/2 cups	crème fraîche (page 187)	375 mL
1/2 cup	whipping cream	125 mL
1/4 cup	fruit sugar	50 mL
1 tsp	pure vanilla extract	5 mL
1 cup	crushed praline (page 115)	250 mL
	Chocolate Filling and Icing	
1-1/2 cups	crème fraîche	375 mL
12 oz	bittersweet or semisweet chocolate, chopped	375 g
	Topping	
1 cup	whipping cream	250 mL
1 cup	coarsely chopped praline	250 mL

1. Preheat oven to 250° F (130° C). Line a jelly roll pan with parchment paper.

2. Beat egg whites with cream of tartar until light. Gradually add 1/2 cup (125 mL) fruit sugar. Beat whites until stiff.

3. In separate bowl, combine remaining fruit sugar, nuts and cornstarch. Fold into meringue. Quickly spread egg white mixture evenly over prepared pan.

4. Bake for 2 hours, turn off oven and leave meringue in oven for 1 hour until meringue is dry. Remove from oven, loosen parchment around the sides and invert. Peel off paper. Carefully cut meringue across width into four equal strips.

5. Meanwhile, to prepare praline filling, combine 1-1/2 cups (375 mL) crème fraîche, 1/2 cup (125 mL) whipping cream and 1/4 cup (50 mL) fruit sugar together. Add vanilla and beat until stiff. Fold in crushed praline. Refrigerate.

6. For the chocolate filling, heat 1-1/2 cups (375 mL) crème fraîche almost to boil. Pour over chopped chocolate and allow to rest for 1 minute. Stir until chocolate melts. Cool to room temperature.

7. To assemble cake, line serving platter with waxed paper strips (see page 37). Place one meringue layer on top and coat with a *thin* layer of chocolate filling. Spread with one-third of praline filling. Repeat, ending with a layer of meringue. Coat top and sides with remaining chocolate mixture. Refrigerate overnight.

8. Just before serving, whip 1 cup (250 mL) whipping cream. Pipe decoratively on top of cake and sprinkle with pieces of praline.

Pound Cake

*T*HIS *is a great basic pound cake. It freezes well and can be used for all sorts of different cakes, trifles and even bread puddings made with cake rather than bread.*

YIELD: One 9 × 5 inch (2 L) cake

1 cup	unsalted butter	250 mL
1-1/2 cups	granulated sugar, divided	375 mL
5	eggs, separated	5
1 tsp	pure vanilla extract	5 mL
	Finely grated peel of 1 lemon	
2 cups	cake and pastry flour, sifted	500 mL
1/4 tsp	cream of tartar	1 mL

1. Preheat oven to 350° F (180° C). Butter a 9 × 5 inch (2 L) loaf pan well and line with parchment paper (see page 36).

2. In large bowl, cream butter until smooth and light. Add 1 cup (250 mL) sugar gradually, beating constantly. Add egg yolks, one at a time, beating after each addition. Add vanilla and lemon peel.

3. Stir flour into batter only until blended.

4. In separate bowl, beat egg whites with cream of tartar until light. Gradually beat in remaining 1/2 cup (125 mL) sugar and continue beating until whites are quite firm. Fold beaten egg whites into batter.

5. Pour batter into pan and bake for 1-1/4 to 1-1/2 hours, or until cake slightly comes away from sides of pan. Cool in pan for 10 minutes. Turn onto cooling rack.

Mocha Cake

WHEN I was growing up in Toronto, there was only one French bakery that I remember clearly. It was located at St. Clair and Yonge and was called the Patisserie Française, I think. Their cakes were very expensive and very rich, and we were only allowed to have them on special occasions.

I remember that this bakery had two styles of cakes. One was a mocha buttercream with cake layers, and one was the same buttercream with meringue layers. My favorite was the one with cake. This is the closest I have ever come to reproducing it — the bakery closed long before I even thought to "study" it.

If your buttercream separates when you are beating it, it may come back on its own if you simply continue to beat; if that doesn't work, beat in a tablespoon or two of vegetable shortening to bring it back together. Use the shortening only if necessary, as it dilutes the marvelous taste of the butter.

A Genoise is a classic French cake. It can be baked as suggested below or baked on a jelly roll pan and used for a roulade or petits fours.

	Genoise Cake	
6	eggs	6
3/4 cup	granulated sugar	175 mL
1 tsp	pure vanilla extract	5 mL
1 cup	cake and pastry flour	250 mL
1/3 cup	unsalted butter, melted and cooled	75 mL
	Buttercream	
1 cup	granulated sugar	250 mL
3/4 cup	extra-strong coffee	175 mL
7	egg yolks	7
1-1/2 cups	unsalted butter, at room temperature	375 mL
2 tbsp	coffee liqueur, optional	25 mL
	Rum Coffee Syrup	
3/4 cup	extra-strong coffee	175 mL
1/3 cup	granulated sugar	75 mL
1/3 cup	dark rum	75 mL
	Filling and Topping	
1/2 cup	apricot jam	125 mL
1-1/2 cups	finely chopped toasted hazelnuts	375 mL
1/3 cup	chocolate coffee beans, optional	75 mL

1. Preheat oven to 350° F (180° C). Butter three 8 inch (20 cm) cake pans and line with rounds of parchment paper. Butter again and dust lightly with flour.

2. Beat eggs with 3/4 cup (175 mL) sugar in a heavy mixer until very light and tripled in volume, about 8 to 10 minutes. Beat in vanilla. Sift flour in three additions over the egg mixture and gently fold in. Fold in melted butter thoroughly.

3. Divide batter among prepared pans. Bake for 25 to 30 minutes, or until cakes are golden and just barely coming away from sides of pan. Remove cakes from pans immediately and cool on wire racks.

4. Meanwhile, prepare buttercream. Combine 1 cup (250 mL) sugar and coffee in a medium saucepan and bring to a boil. Cool until mixture reaches 234° F (112° C) on a candy thermometer (about 5 to 6 minutes). Cool for 1 minute.

5. Beat egg yolks until very light. Slowly, while the beaters are beating, drizzle the coffee syrup into the egg yolks. Continue to whip until mixture is very light and "whipped" looking. Mixture should now be cool. Beating on medium speed, add about one tablespoon soft butter at a time until all the butter is used. Beat in liqueur. The buttercream should be very smooth and creamy. (If it has separated, beat in a bit of shortening to bring it back together.) If buttercream is too soft, refrigerate until spreadable.

6. For the rum syrup, combine coffee and 1/3 cup (75 mL) sugar in a saucepan and cook for 3 minutes. Stir in rum.

7. Warm the apricot jam slightly so that it will spread easily.

8. Drizzle coffee-rum syrup over the cake layers until all the syrup is used.

9. To assemble cake, line a serving plate with strips of waxed paper (see page 37). Place one layer of cake (completely cooled) in the center. Spread with a few tablespoons of jam. Spread with about one-fifth of the buttercream. Repeat with second layer of the cake. Top with third cake layer and then spread a very thin coating of the jam over the top and sides of cake. (This makes the cake easier to ice.) Save a little of the buttercream for piping and spread the remaining over top and sides of cake. Press nuts into sides of cake. Pipe remaining buttercream attractively over the top. Sprinkle or arrange chocolate coffee beans on top. Keep cake refrigerated but allow to stand at room temperature for 30 minutes before serving.

Coffee Hazelnut Dacquoise

YIELD: Serves 12 to 16

*T*HIS *is definitely a special-occasion cake. The coffee filling is so good you can use it as a filling for chocolate cups or to fill and frost a genoise cake (see page 44). If you refrigerate or freeze this cake overnight before serving, the meringue layers will soften and turn more "cakey." If you like crunchy meringues, serve just after assembling — the cake will be a bit crumbly, but will taste just fine.*

You can also omit the chocolate coffee beans and decorate the top of this cake with chocolate fettuccine (see page 125) dusted with icing sugar.

	Meringues	
6	egg whites	6
1 cup	fruit sugar, divided	250 mL
1 tsp	pure vanilla extract	5 mL
1/2 tsp	pure almond extract	2 mL
1 tbsp	cornstarch	15 mL
1 cup	chopped toasted hazelnuts	250 mL
	Filling	
1 cup	unsalted butter	250 mL
1-1/2 cups	sifted icing sugar	375 mL
3	egg yolks	3
1/2 tsp	pure almond extract	2 mL
3 tbsp	coffee liqueur	50 mL
2 tbsp	instant coffee powder	25 mL
1/2 cup	chopped toasted hazelnuts	125 mL
1/2 cup	chopped bittersweet or semisweet chocolate	125 mL
	Topping	
2 cups	whipping cream	500 mL
2 tbsp	coffee liqueur	25 mL
2 tbsp	hazelnut or almond liqueur	25 mL
2 tbsp	sifted icing sugar	25 mL
1/2 cup	chocolate coffee beans, optional	125 mL
1 cup	chopped toasted hazelnuts	250 mL

1. Preheat oven to 300° F (150° C). Butter and flour two large baking sheets. Trace two 8 inch (20 cm) circles on one baking sheet and one on the other.

2. To make meringues, beat egg whites until light. Gradually beat in 1/2 cup (125 mL) fruit sugar. Beat in vanilla and almond extracts.

3. Combine remaining fruit sugar with cornstarch and chopped hazelnuts and fold into egg whites.

4. Spread meringue evenly over the three circles. If you have extra meringue, pipe or spoon it into cookie shapes on the baking sheet. You can eat the cookies or crush them to decorate the sides of the cake in place of the nuts.

5. Bake for 2 to 2-1/2 hours, or until meringues just begin to brown. Turn off oven but leave meringues in oven to cool and dry. Reserve.

6. Prepare filling by beating butter until light. Beat in icing sugar gradually and then add egg yolks one at a time. Beat in almond extract.

7. In small saucepan, warm coffee liqueur and stir in instant coffee powder. Cool. Beat into egg-yolk mixture. Fold in chopped nuts and chocolate.

8. To make topping, whip cream until light. Add liqueurs and sugar and whip until stiff.

9. Assemble cake by spreading half of filling on one meringue. Top with second meringue, spread on remaining filling and cover with third meringue layer. Be careful not to crack meringues. Spread or pipe topping attractively over the entire cake.

10. Sprinkle top with chocolate coffee beans and press chopped nuts or the extra crushed meringue cookies into the sides of the cake.

A Lighter Side: Omit the topping, and dust the top of the cake with sifted icing sugar. Use half the filling.

Margarita Mousse Cake

YIELD: Serves 10 to 12

*T*HIS *is a recipe I developed for* House and Home *magazine, for an article on Southwestern cooking. It was a great success. It's a wonderful treat to have your Margaritas for dessert. You can imitate the drink even further by serving it on glass plates with the rims rubbed with half a lime and then dipped in sugar. Cacti can be piped out of chocolate to garnish the whipped cream for an even more sensational presentation.*

	Crust	
1-1/4 cups	Graham cracker crumbs	300 mL
1/3 cup	unsalted butter, melted	75 mL
	Filling	
1-1/2	envelopes unflavored gelatin	1-1/2
3 tbsp	cold water	50 mL
2	eggs	2
3	egg yolks	3
1-1/2 cups	granulated sugar	375 mL
1 cup	fresh lime juice	250 mL
1 tbsp	finely grated lime peel	15 mL
1/3 cup	tequila	75 mL
1/3 cup	orange liqueur	75 mL
1/3 cup	unsalted butter	75 mL
1 cup	whipping cream	250 mL
	Topping	
1 cup	whipping cream	250 mL
4 oz	bittersweet or semisweet chocolate	125 g

1. Combine crumbs with butter and pat into bottom of 9 inch (23 cm) springform pan. Refrigerate.

2. In a small saucepan, sprinkle gelatin over water. Allow to rest for 5 minutes. Heat gently until gelatin dissolves.

3. In a large saucepan, beat eggs with egg yolks. Whisk in sugar and beat until lemony and light. Whisk in lime juice and peel. Cook gently, stirring constantly, until mixture thickens. Add dissolved gelatin and liqueurs. Cook just until well combined. Add butter and cook just until melted. Transfer mixture to a large bowl and cool to room temperature.

4. Whip cream until light. Fold into custard mixture. Spoon gently into prepared pan. Refrigerate.

5. For the topping, whip cream until firm. Pipe or spoon around edge of cake. Refrigerate cake for at least 4 hours or overnight before serving.

6. For the chocolate cacti, melt chocolate in a bowl over simmering water. Transfer to a clean plastic squeeze bottle. Line a baking sheet with waxed paper. Carefully "pipe" chocolate into cactus shapes on baking sheet. Refrigerate until they harden. Remove gently and place on cake.

A Lighter Side: Use egg whites instead of whipping cream. Beat three egg whites until light. Add 1/4 cup (50 mL) granulated sugar. Fold the beaten egg whites into the custard mixture. Omit the butter in the filling.

Angel Food Cake

A NGEL food cake is making a big comeback; this version is a classic. Light and high, it is perfect plain, with fresh fruit for a "low-calorie" dessert, or as the perfect foil for any number of high-calorie sauces and ice cream concoctions.

Egg whites freeze very well (see page 19), and this recipe is one of the best ways to use them up. The number of egg whites in 2 cups (500 mL) will vary according to the size of your eggs; in this recipe it is better to measure them than to guess.

YIELD: Serves 10 to 12

1-1/2 cups	granulated sugar, divided	375 mL
1 cup	cake and pastry flour	250 mL
2 cups	egg whites	500 mL
1 tsp	cream of tartar	5 mL
1 tsp	pure vanilla extract	5 mL

1. Preheat oven to 375° F (190° C).

2. Sift 3/4 cup (175 mL) sugar with flour twice. Reserve.

3. With an electric mixer, beat egg whites with cream of tartar on medium speed until "loosened." Turn speed to medium-high and continue to beat until light. Slowly add remaining 3/4 cup (175 mL) sugar, beating constantly. (Egg whites should be very light.) Beat in vanilla.

4. Gently mix or fold in flour mixture in three additions. Do not overfold, as you do not wish to deflate the egg whites.

5. Very delicately spoon or pour batter into ungreased 10 inch (4 L) tube pan.

6. Bake for 35 to 45 minutes, or until a cake tester comes out clean and dry, and the top of cake springs back when lightly touched.

7. Leave cake in pan. If pan does not have "little feet" to act as a rack, invert cake (in pan) onto a rack so that air can circulate underneath.

8. To remove cake from pan, use a long thin knife to loosen edges of cake from pan. If pan has a removable bottom, remove side and then loosen bottom with a knife. If pan is in one piece, use a spatula or knife to loosen bottom. (Do not worry if it seems like you are crushing the cake — it usually springs back into shape.)

Pistachio Triangle Cake

YIELD: Serves 8 to 10

I make this cake in many different ways. Sometimes I roll it up like a traditional jelly roll; other times I cut it into strips and roll the strips around one another on a serving platter so that the finished cake is a like a large spiral (see page 72). Although I have been making this cake for years, it was revived by one of my students, Isobel Johnson, who reconstructed it in the triangle shape.

You can also make this cake with hazelnuts or almonds.

	Cake	
1-1/2 cups	shelled pistachio nuts, toasted and ground	375 mL
1 tsp	baking powder	5 mL
5	eggs, separated	5
3/4 cup	granulated sugar	175 mL
2 tbsp	icing sugar	25 mL
	Filling	
2 cups	whipping cream	500 mL
3 tbsp	orange liqueur	50 mL
2 tbsp	icing sugar	25 mL
1/2 cup	chopped candied orange peel	125 mL
3 oz	bittersweet or semisweet chocolate, chopped	90 g
	Garnish	
2 cups	fresh strawberries	500 mL

1. Preheat oven to 350° F (180° C). Line a jelly roll pan with parchment paper and butter and flour lightly.

2. To make cake, combine nuts with baking powder.

3. In large bowl, beat egg yolks with 1/2 cup (125 mL) sugar until lemony. Beat in nut mixture. Reserve.

4. In separate bowl, beat egg whites until light. Then beat in remaining sugar gradually. Gently fold whites into nut mixture.

5. Spread batter evenly over pan and bake for 15 to 20 minutes. Cool, sprinkle with icing sugar and invert onto tea towel. Trim dry edges off cake.

6. To make filling, whip cream until light. Add liqueur and icing sugar and beat until stiff. Reserve about one-quarter of cream for a garnish. Add peel and chocolate to remaining cream.

7. Cut cake into three equal lengthwise strips. Place one strip on a long serving platter. Mound the chocolate/orange cream on the strip in a triangular shape. Place the two other strips on the sides of the cream with the edges meeting at the top.

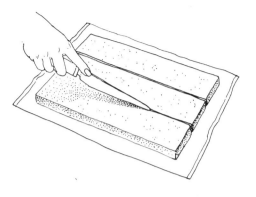
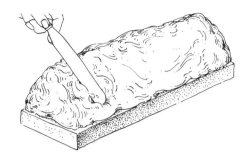

8. Place remaining cream in a piping tube fitted with a small star nozzle and pipe tiny rosettes to cover the "seams."

9. Arrange berries (halve them if they are large) along the sides of the cake. Refrigerate until ready to serve.

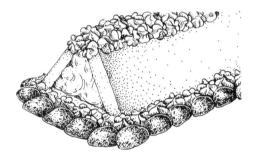

A Lighter Side: Omit the filling. Make the lighter version of the Coconut Mousse (see page 157), Margarita Mousse (see page 48) or Cappuccino Mousse (see page 161). Chill until thickened and almost set. Use in place of the whipped cream filling.

Chocolate Carrot Cake

YIELD: Serves 16
to 20

*T*HIS *is a delicious twist on a carrot cake. Make marzipan carrots for a decoration by coloring 8 oz (250 g) marzipan with orange food coloring (I prefer the paste food colorings, as their colors are very intense); color 2 oz (60 g) marzipan with green food coloring. Shape the orange mixture into tiny carrots and the green mixture into the carrot "tops." Place a marzipan carrot on each square of cake.*

1/2 cup	walnut pieces, toasted	125 mL
1/3 cup	unsweetened grated coconut	75 mL
1/2 cup	raisins	125 mL
1-3/4 cups	all-purpose flour	425 mL
3/4 cup	cocoa	175 mL
1-1/2 tsp	baking powder	7 mL
1 tsp	baking soda	5 mL
1-1/2 tsp	ground cinnamon	7 mL
1/4 tsp	ground nutmeg	1 mL
pinch	allspice	pinch
3	eggs	3
3/4 cup	brown sugar	175 mL
3/4 cup	granulated sugar	175 mL
3/4 cup	vegetable oil	175 mL
4 oz	bittersweet or semisweet chocolate, melted	125 g
1 lb	carrots, peeled and grated	500 g
	Chocolate Cream Cheese Icing	
8 oz	cream cheese	250 g
4 oz	bittersweet or semisweet chocolate, melted	125 g
2 cups	sifted icing sugar	500 mL

1. Preheat oven to 325° F (160° C). Butter a 13 × 9 inch (3.5 L) baking dish and line bottom with parchment paper if you wish.

2. In small bowl, combine walnuts, coconut and raisins. Reserve.

3. In separate bowl, sift or mix together flour, cocoa, baking powder, baking soda, cinnamon, nutmeg and allspice together well. Mix in walnut mixture.

4. In large bowl, beat eggs and blend in brown and granulated sugars gradually. Slowly add oil, blending well. Beat in 4 oz (125 g) melted chocolate. Stir in carrots.

5. Add dry ingredients all at once. Blend only until mixture is evenly combined. Do not overmix.

6. Pour into prepared pan and bake for 35 to 40 minutes, or until top springs back when gently pressed. Cool for 15 minutes and invert (or serve from pan). Remove paper if using.

7. For icing, beat cheese until light. Beat in 4 oz (125 g) melted chocolate. Add icing sugar slowly, beating well until light and spreadable. Spread icing over cooled cake. Mark cake into serving squares and place a marzipan carrot on each.

Lemon Sponge Cake

I love this cake's light texture and gentle lemon flavor. It can be used instead of an angel food cake and as a base for fruit sauces, caramel sauce or even a large cake-style strawberry shortcake.

YIELD: Serves 10 to 12

1-1/3 cups	cake and pastry flour	325 mL
1/2 tsp	baking powder	2 mL
1/4 tsp	salt	1 mL
5	eggs, separated	5
1/2 cup	cold water	125 mL
1 tbsp	lemon juice	15 mL
1-1/2 cups	granulated sugar	375 mL
1 tsp	finely grated lemon peel	5 mL
1 tsp	pure vanilla extract	5 mL
1 tsp	lemon juice	5 mL

1. Preheat oven to 325° F (160° C). Have ungreased tube pan at hand, or three 8 inch (20 cm) layer pans lined with parchment paper circles.

2. Sift together flour, baking powder and salt. Reserve.

3. In large bowl, beat egg yolks with electric mixer until thick and lemony. Beat in ice water and 1 tbsp (15 mL) lemon juice until pale and foamy. Add sugar and beat until very light and sugar is dissolved, about 10 minutes. Add lemon peel and vanilla.

4. Fold flour into yolks in three additions.

5. In separate bowl, beat egg whites with remaining 1 tsp (5 mL) lemon juice until light and fold into batter.

6. Turn batter gently into tube pan and bake for 1 hour, or divide among the three layer pans and bake for 30 minutes. Invert to cool before removing from pan.

Mark's Fishy Birthday Cake

YIELD: Serves 16 to 20

*A*FTER *the success of Anna Banana's birthday party, I decided theme parties were great. My son, Mark, loves fish (not to eat, unfortunately), so for his third birthday, my whole "sophisticated" staff (especially Julie Lewis and Sue Roberts) looked for funny candies to make this cake even more outrageous. (It became a topic of conversation in certain circles that Bonnie's cakes were getting a little weird now that she had children!) This is a large slab of cake that can be cut into any number of shapes. Make a pattern first.*

You can decorate this cake any way you like. We outlined the fish with thin red licorice ropes and used a licorice allsort for the eye and jujubes for the lips. Then we added worm jellies for the tail, jelly beans for the fins and candied fruit slices for the scales.

	Cake	
1-1/4 cups	unsalted butter	300 mL
3 cups	granulated sugar	750 mL
6	eggs	6
2 tsp	pure vanilla extract	10 mL
5 cups	all-purpose flour	1.25 L
2 tbsp	baking powder	25 mL
1/2 tsp	salt	2 mL
2-3/4 cups	milk	675 mL
	Orange Icing	
1 cup	unsalted butter	250 mL
3 cups	sifted icing sugar	750 mL
2 tbsp	cream	25 mL
2 tbsp	orange juice	25 mL

1. Preheat oven to 350° F (180° C). Butter a 18 × 12 inch (5 L) baking dish and line bottom with parchment paper.

2. In large bowl, beat butter until light. Gradually beat in granulated sugar. Add eggs one at a time and beat well after each. Beat in vanilla.

3. Sift or mix dry ingredients and add to egg mixture alternately with milk in three or four additions.

4. Pour batter into pan and bake for 30 to 40 minutes. Allow to cool in pan for 15 minutes and then invert.

5. Trace out the shape of a fish and cut out cake. Make fins and tail with trimmings.

6. For icing, beat butter with icing sugar until light. Add cream and orange juice and add more icing sugar if necessary. Ice cake and stick the fins, etc. on with icing. Decorate cake with candies to resemble a fish (see above).

Orange Chocolate Coffee Cake

THIS is my favorite kind of cake. Not too sweet, not too rich, very moist, easy to make and very easy to eat.

YIELD: Serves 10 to 12

1 cup	unsalted butter	250 mL
1 cup	granulated sugar	250 mL
3	eggs	3
1 tbsp	finely grated orange peel	15 mL
1 tsp	pure vanilla extract	5 mL
1-3/4 cups	all-purpose flour	425 mL
1 tsp	baking powder	5 mL
1 tsp	baking soda	5 mL
pinch	salt	pinch
1 cup	buttermilk or sour cream	250 mL
3 oz	bittersweet or semisweet chocolate, melted	90 g
	Syrup	
1/2 cup	orange juice	125 mL
1/2 cup	granulated sugar	125 mL
3 tbsp	orange liqueur or dark rum	50 mL

1. Preheat oven to 350° F (180° C). Heavily butter a 9 inch (3 L) tube or Bundt pan.

2. In large bowl, cream butter until light. Add sugar gradually. Beat in eggs one at a time. Add orange peel and vanilla.

3. In separate bowl, sift or mix together flour, baking powder, baking soda and salt. Add flour mixture to butter mixture in four additions alternately with buttermilk. Beat only until each addition is just mixed in. Begin and end with a flour addition.

4. Place half of batter in another bowl. Stir in melted chocolate. Do not overmix.

5. Place batter in pan in spoonfuls of alternate colors to create a marble effect. Bake for 50 to 60 minutes, until cake springs back when lightly touched and is just beginning to come away from sides of pan. Cool cake for 10 minutes before turning out of pan. Cool on a wire rack.

6. Meanwhile, prepare syrup by combining orange juice and sugar in a small saucepan. Cook for 4 minutes. Stir in liqueur.

7. Place cake on rack over waxed paper. Poke holes in cake with a cake tester or long toothpick. Pour syrup over cake and allow to soak in.

Lemon Mousse Cake with Strawberries and Pistachios

YIELD: Serves 10 to 12

*W*HEN *I saw the play* Tamara *in New York City — an "interactive" play in which theater-goers actually follow the actors from room to room — I was inspired by the buffet table. When my husband's daughter Fara turned thirteen, we had a large family party at our house, and I finally had a chance to recreate it. I arranged a two-tiered dessert table arrayed with vines and flowers. This cake was one of the highlights; my table didn't look exactly like the one in* Tamara, *but it must have been a hit, because my husband said guests were following him around all night!*

	Nut Pastry	
1 cup	all-purpose flour	250 mL
1/3 cup	toasted hazelnuts or pistachio nuts, finely chopped	75 mL
2 tbsp	granulated sugar	25 mL
1/2 cup	unsalted butter, cut into small pieces	125 mL
1	egg yolk	1
1 tbsp	lemon juice	15 mL
2 oz	homemade or commercial sponge cake (page 53)	60 g
	Filling	
4 cups	fresh strawberries	1 L
1	envelope unflavored gelatin	1
1/4 cup	cold water	50 mL
4	egg yolks	4
3/4 cup	granulated sugar, divided	175 mL
3/4 cup	lemon juice	175 mL
1 tbsp	finely grated lemon peel	15 mL
4 oz	cream cheese	125 g
1-3/4 cups	whipping cream	425 mL
	Garnish	
	Chopped toasted pistachio nuts	
	Sifted icing sugar	

1. Preheat oven to 375° F (190° C).

2. To make the pastry, in large bowl, combine flour with nuts and granulated sugar. Cut in butter until it is in tiny bits.

3. Combine egg yolk with lemon juice. Sprinkle over flour mixture and gather dough together into a ball. Roll or press to fit bottom of 9 or 10 inch (23 or 25 cm) springform pan.

4. Bake for 20 to 25 minutes, or until lightly browned. Break sponge cake into small pieces and sprinkle on top of pastry.

5. Reserve eight of the best strawberries for the top. Hull remaining berries. Cut about twelve even-sized berries in half and arrange around edge of pan with cut side of berries pressed against the edge. Arrange remaining berries to fit inside pan with tips pointing up.

6. To make the filling, sprinkle gelatin over cold water in small saucepan. Allow to soften for 5 minutes. Heat gently until dissolved.

7. In medium saucepan, beat 4 egg yolks with 1/2 cup (125 mL) granulated sugar until light. Beat in lemon juice and peel. Cook, stirring constantly, until mixture thickens and just comes to the boil. Stir in dissolved gelatin. Cool.

8. In large bowl, beat cream cheese with remaining 1/4 cup (50 mL) granulated sugar. Beat in cool lemon cream.

9. In separate bowl, beat whipping cream until light. Fold into lemon cream. Pour over berries. Shake pan gently so lemon mixture falls between berries and top is even. Refrigerate for 3 to 4 hours, or until set. Run knife around edge of pan and remove sides. Place cake on serving platter. (Remove springform bottom only if it comes away easily.)

 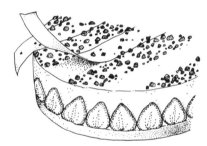

10. Arrange 1 inch (2.5 cm) strips of waxed paper on top of the cake, leaving spaces in between. Sprinkle spaces with pistachio nuts. Remove paper carefully. Leave hulls on reserved berries and cut in half. Arrange berries in rows along empty strips. Dust with icing sugar. Refrigerate until ready to serve.

A Lighter Side: Instead of using the cream cheese and whipping cream, beat 4 egg whites until light. Slowly add 1/4 cup (50 mL) granulated sugar and beat until firm. Fold beaten egg whites into cool lemon custard. Pour over berries.

California Chocolate Pecan Cake

YIELD: Serves 8 to 10

S OMETIMES *it's harder to select the dessert that you want to make for an occasion than it is to actually make the dessert. When The Cookbook Store in Toronto celebrated its fifth anniversary, they asked me to make a birthday cake. I was longing to show off and make a gorgeous rich extravaganza, but I knew the cake would be on display, with people sampling it, for a whole afternoon. I therefore decided to make two of these cakes, because they look pretty, cut easily, don't need refrigeration, and because one large cake would have started to look messy after an hour or two. Alison Fryer and Jennifer Grange reported later that it was a perfect choice.*

The beauty of this cake is that if the glaze isn't perfect, no one will know! Let the glaze run onto the serving platter — it creates a stunning effect and covers any ragged edges. The swirls of white chocolate on the topping hide any imperfections. To finish the presentation, arrange slices of strawberries, kiwi fruit, fresh figs or oranges down the side of each serving.

You can use matzah meal in place of the flour in this recipe and serve the cake at Passover.

6 oz	bittersweet or semisweet chocolate	175 g
3/4 cup	unsalted butter	175 mL
3/4 cup	granulated sugar, divided	175 mL
4	eggs, separated	4
1 cup	ground toasted pecans	250 mL
2 tbsp	all-purpose flour	25 mL
1/4 tsp	cream of tartar	1 mL
	Glaze	
8 oz	bittersweet or semisweet chocolate	250 g
1/2 cup	whipping cream	125 mL
2 oz	white chocolate	60 g

1. Preheat oven to 350° F (180° C). Butter a deep 9 inch (23 cm) cake pan or springform pan and line bottom with a round of parchment paper. Butter lightly again.

2. To make cake, chop bittersweet chocolate and cut up butter. Melt together in a bowl over gently simmering water.

3. In large bowl, beat 1/2 cup (125 mL) sugar with egg yolks until light.

4. Stir in warm chocolate/butter mixture. Mix in pecans and flour.

5. In separate bowl, beat egg whites with cream of tartar until mounds begin to form. Slowly beat in remaining 1/4 cup (50 mL) sugar. Beat until stiff but not dry.

6. Stir one-third of egg whites into chocolate base to lighten it. Fold in remaining whites lightly. Spoon mixture gently into prepared pan.

7. Bake for 35 to 40 minutes, or until a toothpick inserted into the center comes out moist but not runny.

8. Cool cake in pan. Cake will be puffy and then fall, but don't worry.

9. For the glaze, chop bittersweet chocolate and place in a bowl over simmering water with the cream. Heat until melted and smooth. Allow to cool slightly. It should still be pourable.

10. When cake is cool, gently push edges down so the top is flat. Turn cake out onto a serving platter that has a slight lip and leaves a 2 inch (5 cm) border around the cake. (The top of the cake has now become the bottom.) Brush off any crumbs and pour glaze on top of cake. Rotate cake slowly so glaze coats top and sides and excess runs off cake onto platter.

11. Melt white chocolate over simmering water. Pipe chocolate through paper cone or clean squeeze bottle into concentric circles over top of cake. Pipe one or two circles around cake in glaze on platter.

12. With end of chopstick or dull knife, swirl white chocolate and glaze into small circles (see page 31). Serve at room temperature.

Double Fudge Chocolate Cake

YIELD: Serves 10 to 12

*T*HIS *recipe was originally developed for the 1986 Milk Calendar. I always consider it an honor to work on this project because everything is done in the best of taste — the food, photography, food styling and design.*

We heard all kinds of success stories regarding this cake. It was a "bribe" for a hungry doctor, it was sold at $25.00 a cake by a local caterer, and it was delicious even when made by my two preschoolers (the cake was a little messy, but it did still work!). Be sure to use deep cake pans.

4 oz	unsweetened chocolate, chopped	125 g
1/3 cup	cocoa	75 mL
1 cup	boiling water	250 mL
1 cup	unsalted butter	250 mL
2-1/4 cups	granulated sugar	550 mL
3	eggs	3
1 tsp	pure vanilla extract	5 mL
2-1/4 cups	all-purpose flour	550 mL
2 tsp	baking powder	10 mL
1 tsp	baking soda	5 mL
1 cup	milk	250 mL
	Icing	
8 oz	bittersweet or semisweet chocolate, chopped	250 g
1/4 cup	cocoa	50 mL
3/4 cup	milk	175 mL
1/2 cup	unsalted butter	125 mL
3 cups	icing sugar, sifted	750 mL
1-1/2 tsp	pure vanilla extract	7 mL
4 oz	cream cheese	125 g

1. Preheat oven to 350° F (180° C). Butter two deep 9 inch (23 cm) cake pans or springform pans. Line with parchment or waxed paper. Butter again.

2. Place unsweetened chocolate and cocoa in a bowl. Pour boiling water over top. Stir to melt. Cool slightly.

3. In large bowl, cream butter. Beat in sugar gradually. Add eggs one at a time. Beat well after each addition. Beat in vanilla and melted chocolate mixture.

4. In separate bowl, sift flour, baking powder and baking soda. Add to butter mixture alternately with milk, beginning and ending with dry ingredients. Mix ingredients only until blended.

5. Divide batter between pans. Bake for 40 to 45 minutes until center springs back when lightly pressed. Allow to cool in pans for 10 minutes. Invert onto cooling racks.

6. To prepare icing, place bittersweet chocolate, cocoa, milk and butter in top of a double boiler. Heat gently over simmering water just until chocolate melts. Mixture should be smooth. Cool slightly. Beat in icing sugar and vanilla. Chill until spreadable.

7. Combine 1/2 cup (125 mL) icing with the cream cheese. Beat until smooth. Reserve for the decoration.

8. Using the dark icing, sandwich the two layers of cake together. Frost the top and sides. Place cream cheese chocolate frosting in a piping tube and decorate the top and bottom rim of cake as desired.

Chocolate Brownie Pudding Cake

YIELD: Serves 8

*T*HIS *is comfort food at its most comforting — an old-fashioned dessert updated with a strong coffee flavor. The original recipe comes from Jennifer Naldrett's family cookbook. Jennifer works in the cooking school kitchen and is always sharing her own favorites with us. If you are unfamiliar with pudding cakes, this mixture will seem a rather strange concoction. But after it bakes you should have a moist, dark chocolate cake with its own sauce.*

3/4 cup	brown sugar	175 mL
3 tbsp	cocoa	50 mL
1 cup	extra-strong coffee	250 mL
	Cake	
3/4 cup	cake and pastry flour	175 mL
2 tbsp	cocoa	25 mL
1 tsp	baking powder	5 mL
1	egg	1
1/3 cup	granulated sugar	75 mL
3 tbsp	unsalted butter, melted	50 mL
1/3 cup	light cream	75 mL
1 tsp	pure vanilla extract	5 mL

1. Preheat oven to 350° F (180° C). Butter an 8 inch (2 L) square baking dish.

2. Combine brown sugar with 3 tbsp (50 mL) cocoa and coffee. Stir until dissolved. Reserve.

3. Sift flour with 2 tbsp (25 mL) cocoa and baking powder. Reserve.

4. In large bowl, combine egg with sugar, melted butter, cream and vanilla.

5. Stir flour mixture into egg mixture. Spread in prepared pan. Pour coffee mixture on top.

6. Bake for 25 minutes. Serve from the pan, warm or at room temperature, plain or with whipped cream or ice cream.

A Lighter Side: Use milk instead of cream in the cake batter.

Chocolate Chestnut Torte

*T*HIS *moist, chocolaty cake takes little time to make and even less time to eat! Use the sweetened chestnut spread or puree that is sold in specialty shops. If the tin is larger than 8 oz (250 g), you can freeze any leftovers or, if you like, make two cakes and freeze one.*

    This cake can be served as it is for an elegant look, but can also be garnished with some shredded candied orange peel or candied chestnuts dipped in chocolate.

YIELD: Serves 8 to 10

8 oz	bittersweet or semisweet chocolate, chopped	250 g
1/4 cup	unsalted butter	50 mL
1/2 cup	granulated sugar	125 mL
3	eggs, separated	3
2 tbsp	orange liqueur	25 mL
1 tsp	pure vanilla extract	5 mL
8 oz	chestnut puree or spread	250 g
1/3 cup	all-purpose flour	75 mL
	Glaze	
6 oz	bittersweet or semisweet chocolate, chopped	175 g
1/3 cup	whipping cream	75 mL
2 tbsp	unsalted butter	25 mL
1 tbsp	orange liqueur	15 mL

1. Preheat oven to 325° F (160° C). Butter a deep 9 inch (23 cm) cake pan or springform pan. Line with a circle of parchment paper and lightly butter again.

2. To make torte, melt chocolate over gently simmering water. Stir until smooth. Reserve.

3. In large bowl, cream butter until light. Beat in sugar. Add egg yolks one at a time. Beat in orange liqueur, vanilla, chestnut spread and chocolate. Stir in flour gently.

4. In separate bowl, beat egg whites until firm. Be careful not to overbeat. Stir one-quarter of egg whites into chocolate base and gently fold in remaining whites.

5. Turn batter into prepared cake pan and bake for 45 to 55 minutes, or until cake just begins to come away from sides of pan and springs back in the center when lightly touched. Cool in pan.

6. For the glaze, melt chocolate with cream, butter and liqueur. Stir until smooth.

7. Turn cake out onto a serving platter. Spread top and sides with glaze. (For a beautiful presentation surround base of cake with fresh strawberries.)

CAKES

Italian Chocolate Mousse Cake

YIELD: Serves 12
to 16

*T*HIS is my husband's all-time favorite cake. I try not to make it too often *(because he eats so much of it!), but for his fortieth birthday I thought he deserved one. Giuliano Bugialli was teaching at the cooking school on the night of Ray's birthday and, although I was too busy to organize a party, I did find time to make a cake. I invited Giuliano and a few friends to a restaurant for drinks, appetizers and cake after the class. Because most of our friends, like us, are usually in bed by about ten every night, Ray was sure he was just meeting us for a quick goodbye drink with Giuliano. He was pretty surprised when they brought out this cake, which I had taken over to the restaurant in the afternoon. One of our guests, Irene Tam, who has taken every one of my courses and knows all my recipes, was pretty stunned, too. When the cake was brought out, she nudged me and said, horrified, "Bonnie, they stole your recipe!"*

The cake and mousse can be prepared and assembled a few days ahead of time. Refrigerate or freeze until ready to glaze.

1	9 × 5 inch (23 × 12 cm) pound cake (page 43)	1
1-1/2 cups	extra-strong coffee	375 mL
1/4 cup	granulated sugar	50 mL
1/3 cup	dark rum	75 mL
	Mousse	
12 oz	bittersweet or semisweet chocolate, chopped	375 g
8	egg yolks	8
1/2 cup	dark rum	125 mL
3 cups	whipping cream	750 mL
	Glaze	
8 oz	bittersweet or semisweet chocolate, chopped	250 g
1/2 cup	whipping cream	125 mL
	Topping	
1 cup	whipping cream	250 mL
2 tbsp	dark rum	25 mL
	Fresh strawberries	

1. Trim cake into a rectangular or square shape. Slice thinly. Reserve.
2. Line a 13 × 9 inch (3.5 L) baking dish with plastic wrap.

3. Place the coffee, sugar and 1/3 cup (75 mL) rum in a shallow pan and reserve.

4. Prepare mousse by melting chocolate over gently simmering water.

5. In large bowl, beat egg yolks until light. Beat in melted chocolate and 1/2 cup (125 mL) rum.

6. In separate bowl, whip cream until light. Fold into egg-yolk mixture. Reserve.

7. Dip slices of cake into coffee mixture and arrange in the bottom of the prepared baking dish. Fit slices of cake up the sides of pan. Try to fill in any cracks. Spoon in mousse. Top mousse with remaining cake slices. Cover and refrigerate overnight.

8. For the glaze, melt chocolate with cream over simmering water. Cool slightly.

9. Unmold cake onto large serving platter and glaze top and sides. Chill until firm.

10. To make topping, whip cream until light. Add rum and continue whipping until soft peaks form. Decorate cake with cream and garnish with strawberries. Refrigerate until ready to serve.

A Lighter Side: Use beaten egg whites instead of the whipping cream in the filling. Beat 8 egg whites until light. Slowly add 1/2 cup (125 mL) granulated sugar and beat until firm. In the glaze, use milk instead of cream. Omit the whipped cream topping and decorate glazed cake with fresh strawberries.

Chocolate Fantasy Cake

YIELD: Serves 10
to 12

*W*HEN I first began making this cake, I made long chocolate cigar-like curls *(see page 32) and arranged them all over the top. I then took strips of waxed paper and placed them on the curls, leaving about an inch between each strip. I dusted the top heavily with icing sugar and then very carefully removed the paper. It was a fantastic fantasy. Now, for a change, I dip strawberries in chocolate and place some on top of the cake and the rest around the base. I then drizzle melted white chocolate all over the top. (For more information about chocolate-dipped berries, see page 126.)*

	Meringue Layers	
1/4 cup	cocoa	50 mL
1 cup	icing sugar	250 mL
6	egg whites	6
3/4 cup	granulated sugar	175 mL
	Chocolate Mousse Filling	
10 oz	bittersweet or semisweet chocolate	300 g
3/4 cup	unsalted butter, cut into small pieces	175 mL
6	egg yolks	6
8	egg whites	8
1/4 cup	granulated sugar	50 mL
	Cream Topping	
2 cups	whipping cream	500 mL
1/4 cup	Grand Marnier	50 mL
	Garnish	
8 oz	bittersweet or semisweet chocolate	250 g
2 cups	fresh strawberries	500 mL
2 oz	white chocolate	60 g

1. For meringues, preheat oven to 275° F (140° C). Line two cookie sheets with parchment paper and trace out three 8 inch (20 cm) circles.

2. Sift cocoa and icing sugar and reserve.

3. In large bowl, beat egg whites until light. Very gradually add granulated sugar and beat whites until stiff. Quickly fold in cocoa-sugar mixture. Spoon or pipe mixture evenly over circles.

4. Bake for 2 to 2-1/2 hours until meringues are firm but not too brown. Turn off oven, leave door open and allow meringues to cool in oven. They should be dry. Remove from paper.

5. Meanwhile, prepare mousse. Melt chocolate in top of a double boiler over gently simmering water. Remove from heat and beat in butter. Beat in egg yolks one at a time. Mixture should be cool by now.

6. In bowl, beat egg whites until stiff. Beat in sugar gradually. Fold into chocolate-butter base and refrigerate until ready to use.

7. To assemble cake, place one meringue layer on a waxed paper-lined platter. Spread some mousse over layer, top with another layer, more mousse, then the third layer. Ice cake completely with remaining mousse. Refrigerate for at least 2 hours or overnight. Cake can be frozen at this stage.

8. For the cream topping, whip cream until light, add liqueur and whip until stiff. Pipe or spread decoratively over top of cake.

9. For garnish, melt chocolate. Dip berries into chocolate (see page 126). After dipping, place strawberries on a waxed paper-lined cookie sheet. Allow chocolate to set.

10. Arrange berries on top of cake and place any extra berries around the base.

11. Melt white chocolate. With a spoon or in a clean squeeze bottle, drizzle white chocolate over the berries. Refrigerate until ready to serve.

A **Lighter Side**: Omit the cream topping and decorate the cake with fresh undipped strawberries.

Chocolate Mousse Pâté with Espresso Sauce

YIELD: Serves 10 to 12

*T*HIS is one of my favorite desserts, and this is one of my favorite dessert stories. Jim and Carol White came over for dinner one night and I served this. They both have superb palates, so I was flattered when they asked for seconds. Jim liked the cake so much that he ended up having fourths! The next day he called me and said he had been unable to sleep all night, and it finally dawned on him that it was the espresso coffee in the sauce! I detected a bit of amused annoyance in his voice, so to put everything into perspective, I replied, "Well, no one made you have FOUR helpings!"

So, if you think you are going to have four helpings of this cake, use decaffeinated espresso. You can also make this without the ladyfingers.

4 oz	bittersweet or semisweet chocolate	125 g
4	egg yolks	4
1/2 cup	granulated sugar	125 mL
1 tsp	pure vanilla extract	5 mL
1/2 cup	unsalted butter	125 mL
3/4 cup	cocoa	175 mL
1-1/2 cups	whipping cream	375 mL
18	ladyfingers, commercial or homemade (see page 110) approx.	18
1/4 cup	extra-strong coffee	50 mL
10	fresh strawberries	10
	Espresso Sauce	
1 cup	light cream	250 mL
1 tbsp	ground espresso coffee	15 mL
3	egg yolks	3
1/4 cup	granulated sugar	50 mL
2 tbsp	coffee liqueur	25 mL

1. To make the mousse, melt chocolate in double boiler over simmering water. Cool slightly.

2. Beat egg yolks with sugar until light. Beat in melted chocolate and vanilla.

3. In large bowl, beat butter until creamy. Beat in cocoa. Fold in egg-yolk mixture.

4. In separate bowl, whip cream until light. Fold into chocolate mixture. Reserve.

5. Line an 8 × 4 inch (1.5 L) loaf pan with plastic wrap. Line pan with ladyfingers, cutting them to fit if necessary. Brush with coffee. Spoon in chocolate mousse and arrange remaining ladyfingers on top. Cover with plastic wrap and refrigerate overnight. (Cake can be frozen at this point.)

6. Prepare sauce by heating milk with coffee. Allow it to rest for 5 minutes. Strain through a paper towel-lined sieve.

7. In a small saucepan, beat egg yolks with sugar. Whisk in coffee-flavored milk. Cook gently until slightly thickened. Stir in liqueur. Cool.

8. To serve, unmold cake and cut into slices. Swirl some sauce on dessert plates and place a slice of cake on top. Garnish each serving with a fresh strawberry.

A Lighter Side: Use milk instead of cream in the sauce. Use four egg whites, beaten lightly, in place of the whipping cream in the mousse.

Chocolate Mocha Polka Dot Cake

YIELD: Serves 8 to 10

I love the combination of hazelnuts and coffee. And when the combination appears in a chocolate cake, it's even more appealing! The mocha layer between the glaze and the cake makes this dessert irresistible.

	Cake	
6 oz	bittersweet or semisweet chocolate	175 g
3/4 cup	unsalted butter	175 mL
4	eggs, separated	4
3/4 cup	granulated sugar, divided	175 mL
1 cup	ground toasted hazelnuts	250 mL
2 tbsp	all-purpose flour	25 mL
1/4 tsp	cream of tartar	1 mL
	Mocha Cream	
1/2 cup	unsalted butter	125 mL
3/4 cup	icing sugar, sifted	175 mL
2	egg yolks	2
2 tbsp	coffee liqueur	25 mL
1 tsp	instant coffee powder	5 mL
	Glaze	
6 oz	bittersweet or semisweet chocolate	175 g
1/3 cup	whipping cream	75 mL
2 tbsp	extra-strong coffee	25 mL
1 tbsp	unsalted butter	15 mL

1. Preheat oven to 350° F (180° C). Butter a deep 9 inch (23 cm) springform pan and line with a round of parchment paper. Butter lightly again.

2. To make cake, chop chocolate and cut up butter. Melt together over gently simmering water.

3. In large bowl, beat egg yolks with 1/2 cup (125 mL) granulated sugar until light.

4. Stir in warm chocolate/butter mixture.

5. Combine hazelnuts and flour. Stir into chocolate mixture.

6. In separate bowl, beat egg whites with cream of tartar until mounds begin to form. Slowly beat in remaining 1/4 cup (50 mL) granulated sugar. Beat until stiff but not dry. Stir one-third of the whites into chocolate base to lighten it. Fold in remaining whites lightly. Spoon mixture gently into prepared pan.

7. Bake for 35 to 40 minutes, or until a toothpick inserted into the center comes out moist but not runny. Cool cake in pan. Cake will be puffy and then fall.

8. For the cream filling, beat butter until very light. Slowly beat in icing sugar. Beat in egg yolks.

9. Stir coffee liqueur and coffee powder until dissolved. (Warm mixture slightly if necessary.) Beat into butter mixture.

10. When cake is cool, gently push down the sides until the top is even. Turn cake out onto a serving platter lined with strips of waxed paper (see page 37). The top of the cake has now become the bottom. Brush off any crumbs.

11. Reserve 1/3 cup (75 mL) mocha cream. Spread remaining mocha cream over the top of the cake and level it off as much as possible. Refrigerate for 2 to 3 hours, or until very firm.

12. For the glaze, melt chocolate with cream and coffee until smooth. Stir in butter. Cool.

13. When mocha cream is firm, pour glaze over the top of cake. (Warm it ever so slightly if necessary. It should be thick but pourable.) Rotate cake slowly so that glaze coats top and sides. Use a spatula to help spread it.

14. When glaze is set, place reserved mocha cream in clean plastic squeeze bottle or pastry tube fitted with tiny plain nozzle. Pipe polka dots over top and sides of cake. (The mocha cream can also be swirled on top of the cake.)

Chocolate Soufflé Swirl Cake

YIELD: Serves 8 to 10

*F*OR *this cake, a chocolate soufflé mixture is baked on a cookie sheet and spread with a mocha-flavored cream. Instead of being rolled like a traditional jelly roll, it is cut into strips and shaped in concentric circles to form a round cake (see diagram). The remaining cream is then piped in tiny rosettes all over the top of the cake. It's marvelous!*

	Cake	
2 oz	bittersweet or semisweet chocolate	60 g
6	eggs, separated	6
3/4 cup	granulated sugar, divided	175 mL
1/4 cup	cocoa, sifted	50 mL
1 tsp	pure vanilla extract	5 mL
	Icing sugar, sifted	
	Filling and Topping	
2 cups	whipping cream	500 mL
1/4 cup	granulated sugar	50 mL
2 tbsp	extra-strong coffee	25 mL
2 tbsp	coffee liqueur	25 mL
2 tbsp	instant coffee powder	25 mL

1. Preheat oven to 350° F (180° C). Butter a 15 × 10 inch (2 L) baking sheet. Line with parchment paper, butter again and flour lightly.

2. Melt chocolate in double boiler over gently simmering water and cool slightly.

3. In large bowl, beat egg yolks with 1/2 cup (125 mL) granulated sugar until very light. Beat in cocoa, melted chocolate and vanilla. Reserve.

4. In separate bowl, beat egg whites with remaining sugar until light and firm. Stir one-quarter of whites into chocolate mixture and then gently fold in remaining whites.

5. Spread cake mixture evenly over prepared baking sheet.

6. Bake for 15 to 20 minutes until puffed and firm to the touch. Cool in pan for 10 minutes.

7. Dust cake with sifted icing sugar. Loosen edges of cake with a knife. Turn out onto a clean tea towel. Trim edges of cake if necessary.

8. To make filling and topping, whip cream until light. Beat in 1/4 cup (50 mL) granulated sugar, coffee and liqueur. Spread half the mixture over the cake. Smooth evenly.

9. Cut cake into 1 inch (2.5 cm) strips across the width. Roll up one strip and place in the center of a round serving platter. Roll second strip around first and continue until all strips are used.

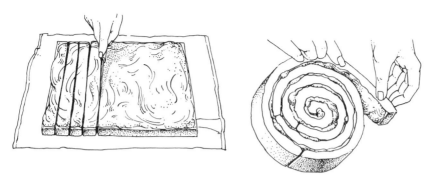

10. Place remaining cream in a piping tube and pipe tiny rosettes over top of cake. Crush coffee if it is in granules and sprinkle lightly over top of cake. Cut into wedges to serve.

A **Lighter Side:** Make the light version of Cappuccino Mousse (see page 161). Chill until thick (the mixture must be almost set to be piped). Use in place of the filling and topping.

Bittersweet Chocolate Cheesecake

YIELD: Serves 10 to 12

I never used to care much for chocolate cheesecakes. Then I met this chocolate cheesecake. The chocolate and cheese flavor are intense. And I am intense about eating it.

If the cake cracks when it is baked or upon cooling, you have probably baked it a bit too long. Do not worry. Make extra glaze and allow it to seep into the cracks.

Crust		
1 cup	chocolate wafer crumbs, about 5 oz (150 g)	250 mL
1/2 cup	finely chopped toasted hazelnuts	125 mL
1/3 cup	unsalted butter, melted	75 mL
Filling		
12 oz	bittersweet or semisweet chocolate	375 g
1-1/2 lb	cream cheese	750 g
1 cup	granulated sugar	250 mL
3	eggs	3
1 tsp	pure vanilla extract	5 mL
1 cup	sour cream	250 mL
Glaze		
4 oz	bittersweet or semisweet chocolate	125 g
1/4 cup	whipping cream	50 mL

1. Preheat oven to 350° F (180° C). Combine chocolate wafer crumbs, nuts and butter. Blend well. Pat into bottom of a 10 inch (25 cm) springform pan. Set aside.

2. Melt 12 oz (375 g) chocolate in the top of a double boiler over gently simmering water. Remove from heat and cool slightly.

3. In large bowl, beat cream cheese until very smooth and light. Gradually beat in sugar. Add melted chocolate and eggs one at a time. Add vanilla and sour cream and stir until thoroughly blended.

4. Spoon mixture into pan and bake for 50 to 55 minutes. Do not worry if cake seems slightly soft — it will firm up when chilled.

5. Remove from oven and run a knife around inside edge of pan. Cool on a rack and then refrigerate.

6. For the glaze, melt 4 oz (125 g) chocolate with whipping cream in double boiler over simmering water and stir until smooth. Cool slightly. Spread over top of cake. Swirl with a knife or use a decorating comb to create concentric circles around the cake. Allow to set. Remove from pan and set on a doily-lined plate. Serve very cold.

A Lighter Side: In the cake, use solid curd pressed cottage cheese instead of the cream cheese. Use yogurt or light sour cream instead of the sour cream. Use half the butter in the crust and omit nuts. Use milk instead of whipping cream in the glaze.

Plum Upside-down Cake

*T*HE *corners of this cake are my favorite pieces. The butterscotch-like topping makes it irresistible.*

You can use apricots or peaches instead of the plums, but peel them before using.

YIELD: Serves 8 to 10

1/4 cup	unsalted butter	50 mL
3/4 cup	firmly packed brown sugar	175 mL
2 lb	plums, preferably purple prune plums, halved and pitted (and sliced if large)	1 kg
	Cake	
1/2 cup	unsalted butter, at room temperature	125 mL
3/4 cup	granulated sugar	175 mL
2	eggs	2
1 tsp	pure vanilla extract	5 mL
1-1/2 cups	all-purpose flour	375 mL
2 tsp	baking powder	10 mL
3/4 cup	milk	175 mL

1. Preheat oven to 350° F (180° C). Place 1/4 cup (50 mL) butter in bottom of 9 inch (2.5 L) square baking dish. Place dish in oven until butter is melted, about 3 to 4 minutes. Sprinkle with brown sugar.

2. Arrange plum halves, cut side down, on top of sugar mixture. Pack them in closely. (If plums are large, slice them.)

3. For the batter, cream 1/2 cup (125 mL) butter in a large bowl until light. Gradually beat in granulated sugar. Add eggs, one at a time, beating well after each addition. Beat in vanilla.

4. In a separate bowl, stir or sift together flour and baking powder. Add to butter mixture alternately with milk, beginning and ending with flour.

5. Spoon batter gently over the fruit.

6. Bake for 40 to 50 minutes. Cool cake on rack for 5 minutes. Invert onto serving tray. Serve warm or cold, with or without ice cream or whipped cream.

CAKES

75

Pumpkin Cheesecake

YIELD: Serves 10 to 12

THIS is a great change from traditional pumpkin pie. Although I do not usually like whipped cream on cheesecakes, it is perfect on this one.

I once made this on Dini Petty's "Cityline." The cake I made ahead of time (that everyone would see) cracked like the Grand Canyon down the center; the one I made on the show (no one saw the finished version) was absolutely perfect! Of course, I just said I had cracked the cake on purpose so no one would feel badly if it happened to them!

You can use cooked pureed pumpkin or unseasoned canned pumpkin in this recipe.

	Crust	
1-1/2 cups	Graham or gingersnap crumbs	375 mL
1/3 cup	unsalted butter, melted	75 mL
	Filling	
1-1/2 lb	cream cheese	750 g
3/4 cup	brown sugar	175 mL
4	eggs	4
1/4 cup	all-purpose flour	50 mL
1/2 cup	whipping cream or sour cream	125 mL
2 tsp	pure vanilla extract	10 mL
1-1/2 cups	pureed cooked pumpkin	375 mL
1 tsp	ground cinnamon	5 mL
1/4 tsp	ground ginger	1 mL
1/4 tsp	ground nutmeg	1 mL
	Topping	
1 cup	whipping cream	250 mL
2 tbsp	icing sugar	25 mL
1 tbsp	dark rum	15 mL
1/4 cup	chopped candied ginger	50 mL

1. Preheat oven to 350° F (180° C). Combine cookie crumbs with melted butter and press firmly into bottom of 10 inch (25 cm) springform pan.

2. In large bowl, cream cheese until smooth. Slowly beat in brown sugar. Add eggs one at a time, beating well after each addition. Beat in flour, then cream and vanilla.

3. In separate bowl, mix pumpkin with spices. Blend into cheese base. Pour mixture into pan.

4. Bake for 1 hour, or until just set. Cool and then chill for 4 hours or overnight. Remove cake from pan and set on serving platter.

5. To make the topping, whip cream until light. Add icing sugar and rum. Beat until thick. Spoon or pipe cream on top of cake and sprinkle with candied ginger.

A Lighter Side: Use solid curd pressed cottage cheese instead of cream cheese. Use light sour cream instead of whipping cream in the filling. Omit the topping and simply dust with icing sugar. (The cake will be slightly more watery.)

Tiramisu Cheesecake Trifle

*T*HERE *are many versions of tiramisu, the popular Italian dessert meaning "lift me up." (There is a more complex recipe on page 171.) This one was a big hit in our cheesecake class because it was so easy to prepare and tasted so great. Make it a day ahead and try to find the mascarpone cheese. It tastes a little like solid crème fraiche and really adds a flavor and texture all its own to desserts or sauces. If you cannot find it, use half cream cheese and half well-drained ricotta.*

YIELD: Serves 8 to 10

12 oz	Italian amaretti biscuits or macaroons	375 g
1/2 cup	extra-strong coffee	125 mL
1/4 cup	dark rum, divided	50 mL
2/3 cup	granulated sugar, divided	150 mL
1 lb	mascarpone cheese	500 g
1-1/2 cups	whipping cream	375 mL
4 oz	bittersweet or semisweet chocolate, finely chopped	125 g
12	fresh strawberries	12

1. Line the bottom of a 12 cup (3 L) glass or attractive bowl with amaretti biscuits or macaroons.

2. Combine coffee with half the rum. Stir in half the sugar. Sprinkle half of this mixture over the biscuits.

3. In large bowl, beat cheese with remaining rum.

4. In separate bowl, whip cream with remaining sugar until light. Fold into cheese mixture.

5. Spread half the cheese mixture over the biscuits. Place another layer of biscuits over the cheese. Sprinkle over remaining coffee. Spread with remaining cheese.

6. Sprinkle chocolate all over the top surface. Refrigerate for 6 hours or overnight. Serve with strawberries as a garnish.

Caramelized Apple Cheesecake

YIELD: Serves 10 to 12

B *ECAUSE caramel is my favorite flavor, it's only natural that I adore this cheesecake. I also love it made with pears — Bartletts are the best ones to use. Always run a knife around a cheesecake as soon as it is baked, so that as it contracts and cools, it will not stick to the edge of the pan and crack.*

	Crust	
1 cup	all-purpose flour	250 mL
2 tbsp	granulated sugar	25 mL
1/2 cup	unsalted butter	125 mL
2	egg yolks	2
	Filling	
1-1/2 lb	cream cheese	750 g
3/4 cup	granulated sugar	175 mL
3	eggs	3
1 tbsp	finely grated orange peel	15 mL
1 tsp	pure vanilla extract	5 mL
	Apples	
6	apples, preferably Spy or Golden Delicious	6
2 tbsp	unsalted butter	25 mL
3/4 cup	granulated sugar	175 mL
	Topping	
1/2 cup	all-purpose flour	125 mL
1/4 cup	granulated sugar	50 mL
1 tsp	ground cinnamon	5 mL
1/3 cup	unsalted butter	75 mL
2 tbsp	sifted icing sugar	25 mL

1. Preheat oven to 350° F (180° C).

2. To make crust, combine flour with granulated sugar. Cut in butter until it is in tiny pieces.

3. Beat egg yolks together and mix into flour mixture until dough forms a ball. Press into the bottom of an unbuttered 9 or 10 inch (23 or 25 cm) springform pan. Bake for 20 minutes. Cool.

4. Meanwhile, to make filling, beat cream cheese with granulated sugar in large bowl. Beat in eggs, orange peel and vanilla. Reserve.

5. When crust has cooled slightly, pour in cheese mixture and return to oven for 45 to 55 minutes, or just until set.

6. Meanwhile, peel, core and slice apples.

7. Melt butter in a large skillet. Add granulated sugar. Watching closely, allow sugar to brown. (If sugar burns, begin again.) Add apples and cook, uncovered, until tender, about 15 to 25 minutes. Reduce until mixture is quite thick — cooking time will depend on how juicy apples are, but the mixture should be like a very thick, chunky applesauce. Cool.

8. Prepare topping by combining flour, granulated sugar and cinnamon in bowl. Cut in butter until mixture is crumbly.

9. When cake comes out of oven, cool for 10 minutes. Spread with apple mixture and sprinkle with topping. Place under broiler until browned, about 2 minutes. Watch closely to make sure it doesn't burn. Cool.

10. Dust with icing sugar. Chill well before serving.

A **Lighter Side**: Use solid curd pressed cottage cheese instead of the cream cheese.

Hazelnut Orange Cheesecake

YIELD: Serves 10 to 12

*T*HIS *is a very dense, crustless cheesecake. You can use almonds, pistachios or pecans instead of the hazelnuts. And if you do not like nuts of any kind, omit them and add 1/4 cup (50 mL) lemon juice and 1 tbsp (15 mL) grated lemon peel along with the orange juice and peel.*

Grind the nuts until they are fine and floury (see page 21).

I love this cheesecake plain, but it is fancier and also delicious when served with a raspberry sauce (page 179). I also sometimes top it with a chocolate glaze and decorate it with strawberries. The perfect pan for this cake is a 3 inch (7.5 cm) deep, 8 inch (20 cm) round cake pan (or "cheesecake" pan, as it is sometimes called). If you do not have one, use an 8 inch (20 cm) springform pan wrapped very well (on the outside only) with heavy-duty foil to prevent leaking when you bake it in a water bath.

1-1/2 cups	hazelnuts	375 mL
2 lb	cream cheese	1 kg
1-1/2 cups	granulated sugar	375 mL
4	eggs	4
1 tbsp	frozen orange juice concentrate, undiluted	15 mL
1 tbsp	finely grated orange peel	15 mL
1 tsp	pure vanilla extract	5 mL
1/2 tsp	pure almond extract	2 mL

1. Preheat oven to 350° F (180° C). Butter a deep 8 inch (20 cm) pan well. Cut a parchment paper circle to fit bottom of pan.

2. Spread hazelnuts on a baking sheet and bake for 8 to 10 minutes until lightly browned and fragrant. Cool. Rub nuts in a tea towel until most of their papery skins come off. (Do not worry if some skins remain.) Grind nuts carefully in a food processor or in a nut grinder. Reserve.

3. In large bowl, beat cream cheese until very smooth. Add sugar gradually and continue to beat well. Add eggs one at a time, beating well after each addition.

4. Beat in orange juice, peel, vanilla and almond extracts. Beat in hazelnuts.

5. Transfer batter to pan. Place in a larger pan and fill with very hot water to come halfway up the sides of the cheesecake pan.

6. Bake for 1-1/4 to 1-1/2 hours, or until the top is lightly browned. If cake is somewhat "loose," do not worry; it will firm up when cool.

7. Remove from water bath and cool, in pan, on a wire rack at room temperature. Turn out of pan onto serving platter, remove parchment paper (and leave cake upside down). Chill overnight before serving.

3

Pies and Pastries

WHEN my students come to me with their pastry woes, it always begins with something like this: "My great aunt has been making pastry for fifty years and she says the secret of making great pastry is to put a little vinegar into the water," or, "My mother's friend is 65 years old and she has been making twelve pies a week her whole life and she says the secret of good pastry is to use lard."

I say the secret is that they have been making pastry for over fifty years, and if you make pastry for fifty years, you'll be an expert, too. The secret is practice, practice, practice. If you make pastry once a week, without even concentrating you'll just naturally get better at it. Just find some tall skinny person to feed it all to. I have to admit that when I first started making pastry I had a lot of problems and fears (see Lemon Meringue Pie, page 96). Here are some tips that helped me get over my pastry fears. I hope they help you, too. If, on the other hand, you make delicious pastry and you do not make it exactly as I have outlined below, don't worry. There are many different ways to do things, and if everyone loves your pies, just keep going.

• Measure the flour and fat in pastry accurately, and leave the liquid as the variable. Sometimes flour varies in dryness, and different amounts of liquid are required.

• I usually use all-purpose flour and butter in dessert pastry. Butter gives pastry an amazing taste and melt-in-your-mouth texture. The aroma is also sensational. The pastry will not be as flaky as one made with lard or shortening, but I feel the other factors are more important, especially if the pastry is to be served cold or at room temperature.

• The liquid and the butter should be cold. Quickly cut the butter into the flour until it is in tiny pieces, like fresh breadcrumbs. You can use a food processor, a pastry blender, two knives, or your fingers.

• Sprinkle the liquid over the "crumbs" and lightly gather the dough together into a ball. If it is too dry, add about 1 tsp (5 mL) more liquid; continue doing this until the mixture stays together well. Knead the dough slightly by smearing the dough away from you with the palm of your hand. Then gather it together; repeat a few times. Gather the dough into a ball once more and then wrap in plastic wrap and refrigerate until you are ready to roll.

• Some chefs believe that dough must be refrigerated and allowed to "relax" before rolling. But unless I feel I have overhandled the dough a lot, I don't worry about it. You can experiment with a taste test and see if you can tell the difference.

• I like to use a long rolling pin on ball bearings to roll out pastry, although some cooks like a straight "pin" style rolling pin. (In a pinch I have used a broom handle or an empty Bordeaux wine bottle.) Marble rolling pins keep the dough chilled, but they are usually small and too heavy. I do not like the rolling pins that contain ice cubes, because water tends to condense on the outside of the pin, wetting the dough.

• I like to use a pastry cloth and rolling pin cover to roll out dough. Flour the cloth and the "stocking" lightly. That way the dough does not stick too much, and you do not have to use too much excess flour. The more you use the cloth, the more seasoned it becomes and the less flour you need. Store the cloth in the refrigerator to avoid flour weevils (they don't hurt you, but they aren't very nice to serve to company). Wash the cloth after using it ten or twelve times, or if it is particularly greasy or dirty. Some people like to use plastic wrap, marble slabs, "target" sheets, etc. Whatever gives you confidence is okay.

• Place the ball of dough in the center of the floured cloth and gently "bang" the dough down to flatten it into a wider circle. Starting at the center, roll away from you toward the outside edge of the pastry. Continue rolling from the center to the outside edge going around clockwise. When your pin reaches the outside edge, allow it to roll off and up, instead of smearing the pastry into the cloth (which prevents the dough from spreading out). Roll the dough as thin as you wish (a thinner pastry will have fewer calories than a thicker pastry, although it may be a bit harder to handle). Hold the pie dish over the circle of pastry to be sure it is large enough.

• To transfer the pastry to the dish, place the rolling pin over the pastry nearest to you. Roll the dough up over the pin and then unroll it over the dish. Press the pastry into the dish gently and trim and crimp the edges.

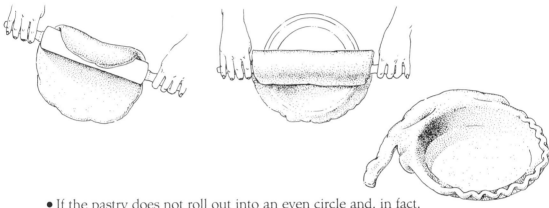

• If the pastry does not roll out into an even circle and, in fact, looks more like a map of Norway with the fjords hanging off the side, don't worry. It won't help. Do not reroll the dough. Rerolling only makes it worse. Just cut the pastry into strips and fit it into the dish, patching the edges together with a bit of cold water.

• Although ideally you should not reroll dough, sometimes, when you are making small tarts, etc., you will have to. In that case, gather up all the scraps of dough but do not knead them together into a ball. Just push them together gently and roll.

Baking Blind

If you are making a single-crust pie, the crust will be less soggy if it is partially baked or baked "blind" before filling. If you just bake the pie shell as is, the crust can bubble up and slip down the sides of the dish. If you prick it first, the pastry can crack and filling can later run through the holes, making the crust even soggier.

Therefore, the ideal solution is to bake a crust blind. Line the pastry with parchment paper, waxed paper or foil (parchment paper is less likely to stick to the pastry when it is removed). Crush the piece of paper into a ball so that it is easier to mold into the pastry shell. If you are using waxed paper, be sure to trim the edges even with the top of the pastry, as waxed paper can burn in the oven. Then fill the shell with dried beans, uncooked rice, legumes or special pie weights. The weights hold the pastry down as it bakes and keeps the sides pushed up. Bake the pastry for 15 to 20 minutes at 425° F (220° C). Then remove the weights and carefully remove the paper. If the filling is not going to be baked, return the empty shell to a 375° F (190° C) oven for 15 to 25 minutes. (Check to make sure the pastry is not browning too much.)

Before adding the filling to the baked or partially baked pastry shell, chefs often "treat" the pastry to further prevent the bottom crust from becoming soggy. There are many ways to do this:

• Brush the bottom crust with lightly beaten egg white. Allow it to dry before filling crust.

• The bottom of the crust can be brushed with jam or jelly.

• Melted bittersweet or semisweet chocolate can be spread over the bottom. Let it dry before filling.

• Caramel can be drizzled over the bottom of the pastry before filling.

• With custard fruit pies or flans, excess liquid can ooze from the pastry cream or fruit and make the crust soggy. The flan certainly would not be great the next day. Some pastry chefs cut a thin circle of sponge cake, place it over the bottom of the crust, then add the pastry cream, fruit and glaze. The sponge absorbs the excess moisture and almost completely disappears. You can do this at home if you must make a flan of this kind a day or two ahead. You can also buy commercial sponge cake or ladyfingers, break them into pieces and just scatter them over the crust before filling it.

Food Processor Pastry

Pastry can be made very easily in a food processor. Just make sure you do not overprocess it. Although cookbooks always go on about overhandling the dough, when you make pastry by hand, unless you reroll or really knead the dough excessively, it's hard to overwork it. But the food processor goes so quickly, it is sometimes hard to control.

Combine the flour with any other dry ingredients in the work bowl fitted with the steel knife. Cut the cold fat into small even pieces and add it to the flour. Process on/off until the fat is in tiny bits. Sprinkle the liquid over the pastry (use the smaller amount indicated in the recipe). Process on/off until the dough comes together and is moist, but is still in many pieces. Remove it from the work bowl and gather together into a ball with your hands.

All-purpose Pastry

I generally hate the term "all-purpose" because it refers to something that is okay with everything but not extra special. But this is an all-purpose special pastry! You can use it for double-crusted pies, tarts and turnovers. I like pastry the best when it is made with all butter. However, if I am making a quiche or something that is to be served hot, I may use half butter and half lard or shortening. The butter will give the pastry flavor, color and a wonderful aroma, and the lard or shortening will make it flakier and a little easier to roll.

YIELD: Enough for one 10 to 12 inch (25 to 30 cm) single-crust pie or one 8 to 9 inch (20 to 23 cm) double-crust pie

2 cups	all-purpose flour	500 mL
1/4 tsp	salt	1 mL
3/4 cup	unsalted butter, cold, cut into pieces	175 mL
1/3 cup	ice water	75 mL

1. Combine flour with salt in a large bowl. Cut butter in until it is in tiny bits.

2. Sprinkle mixture with cold water. Gather together into a ball.

Rich Pastry

YIELD: Enough pastry for one 9 inch (23 cm) open-faced tart

*T*HIS *delicate pastry is so rich and tender, it just melts in your mouth! What better container for fresh raspberries. If the pastry breaks as you are lifting it into the pan, don't worry — just patch. It is worth any amount of trouble. Use this only for very delicate open-faced tarts.*
This is best if it is completely baked before using.

1 cup	all-purpose flour	250 mL
pinch	salt	pinch
1/2 cup	unsalted butter, cold, cut into pieces	125 mL
1 tbsp	lemon juice or white vinegar	15 mL
1 tbsp	ice water, only if necessary	15 mL

1. Combine flour with salt in large bowl. Add butter and cut in until it is in tiny pieces.

2. Sprinkle flour mixture with lemon juice or vinegar and gently gather dough together to form a ball. Knead lightly and, if necessary, sprinkle with a little water.

3. Wrap in plastic wrap and refrigerate for 15 to 30 minutes before rolling out. Bake blind (see page 83) before filling.

Sweet "Cookie" Pastry

YIELD: Enough pastry for one 10 to 12 inch (25 to 30 cm) open-faced tart

*T*HIS *pastry has a cookie-like texture and flavor. It is also prepared more like a cookie, in that the butter used in the pastry should be slightly soft. The pastry is dense rather than flaky.*
When rolling out this dough do not try to roll it too thin, as it will break easily. This pastry is great for cheesecakes, open-faced flans and small tarts.

2 cups	all-purpose flour	500 mL
3 tbsp	granulated sugar	50 mL
pinch	salt	pinch
2/3 cup	unsalted butter, at room temperature	150 mL
1	egg yolk	1
1/3 cup	cold water, approx.	75 mL

1. Combine flour with sugar and salt in large bowl.

2. Rub the butter into the flour until it is partly blended.

3. Combine egg yolk with water and sprinkle over the flour. Smear and knead pastry together until it forms a ball.

4. Wrap in plastic wrap and refrigerate for about 15 minutes before rolling.

Quick Puff Pastry

THIS recipe for puff pastry makes this flaky, buttery crust easily available to all home cooks. It does not puff quite as much as classic puff pastry, but with more and more people busy with other activities, this fast method is overtaking the classic version in many circumstances. It can be used for turnovers, quiches, double- or single-crust pies, and fish or meat wrapped in pastry.

YIELD: Approximately 2 lb (1 kg) dough

2-1/2 cups	all-purpose flour	625 mL
2/3 cup	cake and pastry flour	150 mL
2 cups	unsalted butter, divided	500 mL
1 tbsp	lemon juice	15 mL
1 cup	cold water, approx.	250 mL

1. Combine or sift flours together in large bowl.

2. Cut 1/4 cup (50 mL) butter into flour until it disappears. Cut remaining butter into 1/2 inch (1 cm) cubes. Toss with flour but do not incorporate it at all.

3. Place lemon juice in a cup measure and add cold water to reach 1 cup (250 mL). Sprinkle liquid evenly over flour mixture and gather together loosely. It will be very rough.

4. Turn dough out onto a floured surface and pat into a rough rectangle. Roll dough out into a rectangle approximately 10 inches (25 cm) wide and 20 inches (50 cm) long.

5. Fold long ends of dough into the center and then fold in half like a book. Roll into another rectangle and fold again. Repeat a third time. At any time, if dough is hard to handle, refrigerate it for about 30 minutes before continuing.

6. After the third rolling, wrap dough well in plastic and refrigerate or freeze until ready to use. Use in any recipe that calls for puff pastry.

Harvest Fruit Pie

YIELD: Serves 8

I am particularly fond of the blend of flavors in this pie. I first sampled something like this at Chris Boland's restaurant, Trapper's, in Toronto. This version is more like a traditional apple pie, but it is made with pears and apricots as well! Serve it with a slice of Cheddar cheese or vanilla ice cream. (For a traditional apple pie, use six apples.)

1	recipe All-purpose Pastry (page 85)	1
	Filling	
2	ripe pears, preferably Bartlett	2
3	apples, preferably Spy	3
1/2 cup	dried apricots	125 mL
2/3 cup	granulated sugar	150 mL
3 tbsp	all-purpose flour	50 mL
3 tbsp	unsalted butter, cut into bits	50 mL
2 tbsp	lemon juice	25 mL
1 tbsp	ground cinnamon	15 mL
pinch	ground nutmeg	pinch
	Glaze	
1	egg	1
1 tsp	granulated sugar	5 mL

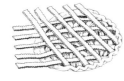

1. Preheat oven to 425° F (220° C).

2. Divide dough into two pieces, one slightly larger than the other. Roll out larger piece to fit a 9 inch (23 cm) pie plate.

3. Peel, halve and core pears and apples. Cut into small pieces. Cut apricots (a pair of scissors works best). Combine fruit with sugar, flour, butter, lemon juice and spices. Spoon into crust.

4. Roll out second piece of dough. Cut into 1 inch (2.5 cm) strips with pastry cutter. Top pie with lattice pattern. Crimp edges.

5. To make glaze, combine egg with sugar and brush on pastry.

6. Bake for 15 minutes. Reduce heat to 350° F (180° C) and bake for 45 minutes longer. Check pie after 30 minutes; if it is browning too much, cover loosely with foil. Cool for at least 30 minutes before serving.

A Lighter Side: Omit bottom crust. Place fruit in an 8 cup (2 L) shallow casserole. Top filling with top crust (make half the pastry or save remaining pastry for another purpose).

Double Blueberry Tart

I have been making this tart for years, ever since Gwen Fargeon, my cooking friend in Montreal, directed me to it. It is rich with the flavor of blueberries, both baked in the filling and fresh on the top! If you love blueberries, this is a must.

YIELD: Serves 8

1	recipe Rich Pastry (page 86)	1
	Filling	
3 cups	blueberries	750 mL
1/4 cup	granulated sugar	50 mL
2 tbsp	all-purpose flour	25 mL
1 tbsp	unsalted butter, cold, cut into bits	15 mL
1/2 tsp	ground cinnamon	2 mL
1 tsp	finely grated orange peel	5 mL
	Topping	
2 cups	blueberries	500 mL
1/2 cup	apricot jam	125 mL
1 tbsp	orange liqueur	15 mL

1. Preheat oven to 425° F (220° C).

2. Roll out pastry to fit a 9 inch (23 cm) pie plate or 10 inch (25 cm) quiche pan. Place pastry in dish. Crimp edges. (Save scraps of dough in case pastry needs patching later.) Line with parchment paper. Fill with pie weights or dried legumes. Bake for 20 minutes. Cool for 5 minutes. Carefully remove pie weights and paper. Cool slightly. (If any of the pastry comes away with the paper, patch with scraps of dough.)

3. Combine blueberries with sugar, flour, butter, cinnamon and orange peel. Spoon into crust. Reduce oven temperature to 375° F (190° C).

4. Bake for 30 to 35 minutes.

5. As soon as pie is finished, while it is hot, arrange uncooked blueberries on top of cooked filling. Heat jam with liqueur and brush over top of blueberries. Serve warm or cold with ice cream or whipped cream if desired.

A Lighter Side: Instead of the Rich Pastry, make half of the All-purpose Pastry recipe (page 85) — use 1 cup (250 mL) flour, pinch of salt, 6 tbsp (90 mL) unsalted butter and approximately 3 tbsp (50 mL) ice water. Serve without whipped cream or ice cream.

Fresh Coconut and Banana Cream Pie

YIELD: Serves 8

THIS is the type of dessert that I always recommend serving in small slices. But it is also the type of thing I could eat all myself! It's heavenly. You can use 2 cups (500 mL) grated coconut instead of the fresh if you prefer. The chocolate on the crust prevents it from going soggy if made a day ahead.

1	medium coconut	1
	Crust	
1-1/4 cups	all-purpose flour	300 mL
1/2 cup	unsalted butter	125 mL
1/4 cup	ice water	50 mL
2 oz	bittersweet or semisweet chocolate	60 g
	Filling	
1	envelope unflavored gelatin	1
1/4 cup	cold water	50 mL
3/4 cup	granulated sugar	175 mL
1/4 cup	cornstarch	50 mL
1 cup	milk	250 mL
3	eggs	3
1 tsp	pure vanilla extract	5 mL
1 cup	whipping cream	250 mL
3	ripe bananas	3
	Topping	
1 cup	whipping cream	250 mL
2 tbsp	granulated sugar	25 mL
2 tbsp	dark rum	25 mL

1. Preheat oven to 350° F (180° C).

2. Crack coconut open by piercing the three "eyes" with a nail and hammer and allowing "milk" to run out. Discard milk or save for another purpose. Holding coconut in one hand, hit coconut with hammer across the middle, rotating coconut constantly. When it cracks, break in half. Dig out the meat carefully with a sharp knife. Peel pieces with a vegetable peeler if you wish (this is not necessary). Grate coconut on a hand grater or with the shredding disc of a food processor.

3. Spread coconut on a baking sheet and toast for 5 to 7 minutes, or until nicely browned. Stir once or twice during baking. Allow to cool. You should have approximately 2 cups (500 mL), but if there is a little more, simply use it up in the filling.

4. Increase oven temperature to 425° F (220° C).

5. For the crust, combine 1/4 cup (50 mL) coconut with the flour. Cut in the butter until it is in tiny pieces. Sprinkle mixture with ice water and gather dough together in a ball.

6. Roll out dough to fit a 9 inch (23 cm) pie dish. Fit into dish and crimp edges of pastry attractively. Line shell with parchment or waxed paper and fill with dry beans or rice.

7. Bake for 15 minutes. Remove beans or rice, remove paper and return crust to oven. Reduce heat to 350° F (180° C) and bake for 15 to 20 minutes longer, or until slightly browned. Cool.

8. Melt chocolate over barely simmering water. Spread pie shell with melted chocolate. Allow to set.

9. For the filling, sprinkle gelatin over cold water in small saucepan. Allow to rest for 5 minutes, then heat gently, stirring, until gelatin dissolves.

10. Meanwhile, in a medium saucepan, combine sugar with cornstarch. Whisk in milk until mixture is smooth. Heat until it comes to a boil and thickens.

11. Beat eggs in a small bowl and add some of the hot custard. Return eggs and custard to the saucepan and cook gently for 3 or 4 minutes. Beat in gelatin and vanilla. Transfer to a bowl and cool to room temperature.

12. Meanwhile, whip cream for the filling until light but not too firm. When lightly whipped, fold cream into the filling along with all but 1/4 cup (50 mL) toasted coconut.

13. Slice bananas. Arrange half of the bananas on the bottom of pie shell. Spoon in half the filling. Arrange remaining bananas on top. Spread with remaining filling.

14. Whip cream for the topping. When light add sugar and rum. Continue to beat until stiff. Pipe or spoon onto the top of the pie and sprinkle the top with remaining coconut. Refrigerate for at least 4 hours or overnight.

A Lighter Side: Omit chocolate coating on crust. Beat 3 egg whites until firm but not dry and use instead of the whipping cream in the filling. Omit cream topping and sprinkle top with toasted grated coconut.

Caramel Cream Pie

YIELD: Serves 8

*F*OR *a caramel-lover, this pie cannot be beat. If you love chocolate, you could fold 1 cup (250 mL) coarsely chopped bittersweet chocolate into the filling and call it Chocolate Chip Caramel Cream Pie.*

1/2	recipe All-purpose Pastry (page 85)	1/2
1 cup	granulated sugar	250 mL
1/2 cup	water, divided	125 mL
1-1/2 cups	whipping cream, divided	375 mL
1	envelope unflavored gelatin	1
3	egg yolks	3
2 tbsp	extra-strong coffee or coffee liqueur	25 mL
	Garnish	
3/4 cup	whipping cream, divided	175 mL
1 tbsp	extra-strong coffee or coffee liqueur	15 mL
1 tbsp	granulated sugar	15 mL

1. Preheat oven to 425° F (220° C).

2. Roll out pastry to fit a 9 inch (23 cm) pie dish. Place pastry in pie dish and trim and crimp edges.

3. Line pastry with parchment paper and weigh down with pie weights.

4. Bake for 15 minutes. Remove weights and paper. Reduce heat to 350° F (180° C). Bake for 15 to 20 minutes longer, until lightly browned. Cool.

5. In a medium or large heavy saucepan, combine sugar with 1/4 cup (50 mL) water. Heat, stirring, until sugar dissolves. Stop stirring. Have a small bowl of cold water and a pastry brush on hand. Brush down sugar crystals from the sides of the pan. Allow mixture to cook until sugar turns a deep caramel color. Be careful not to burn mixture.

6. Remove pan from heat. Standing back and averting your face, pour 1/2 cup (125 mL) whipping cream into the pot. The mixture will bubble up furiously. Return to the heat for a minute to dissolve fully.

7. Sprinkle gelatin over remaining 1/4 cup (50 mL) water in a small saucepan. Allow to rest for 5 minutes and then heat gently until dissolved.

8. In large bowl, beat egg yolks until light. Beat in coffee. Slowly beat in warm caramel mixture and gelatin. Transfer to the saucepan and cook gently until mixture thickens slightly. Transfer to a bowl and cool.

9. When caramel mixture is cool but not yet set, whip remaining 1 cup (250 mL) whipping cream and fold into caramel. Spoon lightly into prepared crust and smooth top. Refrigerate for at least 3 hours or overnight.

10. For the garnish, whip cream until light. Beat in coffee and sugar. Pipe tiny rosettes around outside edge of pie. Refrigerate until ready to serve.

Old-fashioned Rhubarb and Strawberry Pie

*W*HEN *you want to feel like mother earth, try making this pie. Its old-fashioned flavor is always popular. If the rhubarb is home-grown (usually very tart), increase the sugar to 1 cup (250 mL).*

YIELD: Serves 8

1	recipe All-purpose Pastry (page 85)	1
	Filling	
4 cups	diced rhubarb, approx. 1-1/4 lb (625 g)	1 L
2 cups	fresh strawberries, hulled and quartered	500 mL
3/4 cup	granulated sugar, approx.	175 mL
1/3 cup	all-purpose flour	75 mL
2 tbsp	unsalted butter, cut into bits	25 mL
	Glaze	
1	egg yolk	1
2 tbsp	cream	25 mL

1. Preheat oven to 425° F (220° C).

2. Divide dough into two pieces — one slightly larger than the other. Roll the large piece into a circle to fit a 9 inch (23 cm) pie dish.

3. Combine rhubarb with strawberries, sugar, flour and butter. Fill pie shell with rhubarb mixture. Trim edges of pastry, leaving just enough to crimp.

4. To make glaze, combine egg yolk and cream. Brush edges of pastry with glaze.

5. Roll out remaining dough and place on top of pie. Crimp edges together. Cut steam slits in top of pastry. Brush top with remaining glaze.

6. Bake for 15 minutes. Reduce oven temperature 350° F (180° C) and continue baking for 45 to 50 minutes. Cool on rack. Serve with ice cream.

A Lighter Side: Omit the bottom crust. Place filling in an 8 cup (2 L) shallow casserole. Top with the top crust. (Make half the pastry recipe, or reserve the remaining pastry for another use.)

93

Individual Apple Tarts

YIELD: Twelve
6 inch (15 cm) tarts

I usually assemble these tarts ahead of time and bake them about one hour before serving. For a wonderful teatime treat, make "tartlets" 3 inches (7.5 cm) in diameter.

The tarts can be served with a topping made by combining 1 cup (250 mL) whipping cream, lightly whipped, with 1/2 cup (125 mL) sour cream. Sweeten with a little sugar if you wish.

	Pastry	
1-1/2 cups	all-purpose flour	375 mL
1 tbsp	granulated sugar	15 mL
pinch	salt	pinch
3/4 cup	unsalted butter, cold, cut into bits	175 mL
1/4 cup	ice water	50 mL
	Filling	
4	apples, preferably Spy	4
1/4 cup	granulated sugar	50 mL
1/4 cup	unsalted butter, cold, cut into bits	50 mL
1 cup	apricot jelly or jam	250 mL
1 tbsp	orange liqueur or Cognac	15 mL

1. Prepare pastry by combining flour with sugar and salt. Cut in butter until it is in tiny bits. Sprinkle with ice water and gather into a ball. (Add more water only if necessary.) Divide dough in half and roll out each portion. Dough should be about 1/8 inch (3 mm) thick. Cut out 6 inch (15 cm) circles and place on a baking sheet lined with parchment paper. Reroll scraps if necessary. Cover with plastic wrap and refrigerate until ready to use.

2. To prepare filling, peel, halve and core apples. Slice them very thinly. Arrange in a circular pattern on pastry rounds. Sprinkle with sugar, dot with butter and refrigerate until ready to bake.

3. About 1 hour before serving, preheat oven to 425° F (220° C). Bake tarts for 20 to 30 minutes. Check them after 15 minutes and reduce oven temperature if they are browning too much.

4. Heat jam with liqueur. Strain if necessary. Brush on hot tarts.

Cherry "Tartlot"

*T*HIS *huge, luscious tart is sure to be a spectacular hit at a large summer barbecue or dinner party. It can be made with blueberries or strawberries instead of the cherries, and sometimes I use all three for a really pretty effect.*

YIELD: Serves 16 to 20

1	recipe All-purpose Pastry (page 85)	1
1/4 cup	apricot jam	50 mL
2 cups	milk	500 mL
4	egg yolks	4
2/3 cup	granulated sugar	150 mL
1/2 cup	all-purpose flour	125 mL
1	envelope unflavored gelatin	1
1/4 cup	water	50 mL
2 tbsp	Grand Marnier or other orange liqueur	25 mL
1 cup	whipping cream	250 mL
3 lb	fresh cherries, pitted	1.5 kg
1 cup	raspberry jelly	250 mL

1. Roll out dough to fit a large jelly roll pan and drape into the pan. Crimp edges. Refrigerate for 30 minutes.

2. Preheat oven to 425° F (220° C).

3. Line pastry with parchment paper and weigh down with pie weights, dry beans or rice.

4. Bake for 15 minutes. Remove weights and paper. Reduce heat to 375° F (190° C). Bake for 10 to 15 minutes longer, or until lightly browned. Cool. Spread pastry with jam (heat a little if necessary to make spreading easier).

5. Meanwhile, heat milk in small saucepan.

6. In large saucepan off heat, whisk egg yolks with sugar and flour. Whisk in hot milk. Cook, stirring constantly, until mixture comes to a boil and thickens.

7. Sprinkle gelatin over water in a small saucepan and soften for 5 minutes. Heat gently until dissolved. Stir into custard mixture. Add Grand Marnier. Cool to room temperature.

8. Whip cream until light. Fold into cool custard. Spread over cooled pastry.

9. Arrange pitted cherries over top of custard to cover completely. Heat jelly slightly and spoon over cherries. Refrigerate until ready to serve.

A Lighter Side: Use 2 percent milk in the filling, and omit the cream. Reduce flour to 1/4 cup (50 mL).

Lemon Meringue Pie

*W*HEN *I was beginning my chef training, and was still intimidated by pastry, I went out with a sweet guy who could get me to do just about anything with lines like, "Bonnie, you are such a great cook. I just know you could make my favorite dessert better than anyone else." Being very young and naive, I fell for this, and his favorite dessert turned out to be lemon meringue pie. It was a snap, I thought. My mother made gorgeous lemon pies with frozen pastry and lemon pie filling.*

Well, it seems that my boyfriend's mother always made pies from scratch, and he really could tell the difference between a store-bought and homemade crust. So I started making two lemon pies a week. By the end of six months I was sick of lemon pies and also sick of him, and we parted company. But I did learn to make a mean lemon pie.

	Crust	
1-1/4 cups	all-purpose flour	300 mL
1 tbsp	granulated sugar	15 mL
pinch	salt	pinch
1/2 cup	unsalted butter, cold, cut into pieces	125 mL
2 tbsp	ice water	25 mL
1 tbsp	lemon juice, cold	15 mL
	Filling	
4	egg yolks	4
2	eggs	2
1-1/4 cups	granulated sugar	300 mL
2 tbsp	cornstarch	25 mL
1 cup	lemon juice	250 mL
1/2 cup	water	125 mL
1 tsp	finely grated lemon peel	5 mL
1/4 cup	unsalted butter	50 mL
	Meringue	
1/2 cup	granulated sugar	125 mL
4	egg whites	4

1. For the pastry, combine the flour with sugar and salt. Cut in the butter until it is in tiny bits. Sprinkle with water and lemon juice. Gather dough together into a ball (use a little more water if necessary). Roll out dough to fit a 9 inch (23 cm) pie dish. Fit into pie dish gently and trim edges. Crimp crust attractively. Refrigerate until ready to bake.

2. Preheat oven to 425° F (220° C). Line pastry with parchment paper. Fill with pie weights or dried legumes. Bake for 15 to 20 minutes. Remove weights and then paper.

3. Reduce oven temperature to 375° F (190° C). Bake crust for 15 to 20 minutes longer, until nicely browned. Cool on a rack.

4. Meanwhile, prepare filling. In a medium or large saucepan off heat, combine egg yolks with eggs. Whisk in sugar until mixture is light in color and well combined. Whisk in cornstarch. Add lemon juice and water. Combine until smooth. Add peel.

5. Cook mixture, stirring constantly, over medium heat until mixture thickens and comes to the boil. Stir in butter. Cook until butter melts.

6. Remove from heat. Transfer to another bowl (so mixture will cool faster). Cool to room temperature, stirring occasionally.

7. For the meringue, stir sugar into egg whites. Warm mixture over a bowl of hot water until warm to the touch. Beat egg whites until very stiff.

8. To assemble, spread filling in cooled baked pastry shell.

9. Mound meringue gently over the top, making sure meringue touches edges of crust all around (to help prevent shrinking). Swirl meringue into peaks and valleys.

10. Preheat boiler. Place pie under broiler and, watching very closely, brown the top. Cool for at least 1 hour before serving, or refrigerate if keeping longer. (The meringue will cut easily if you dip your knife into very hot water just before slicing.)

Butter Pecan Squares

*T*HESE squares are a cross between a butter tart and a pecan pie. Cut into large squares for dessert, or smaller ones for a snack.

YIELD:
Approximately 32 small squares

1	recipe All-purpose Pastry (page 85)	1
2 cups	toasted pecan halves	500 mL
4	eggs	4
1-1/4 cups	brown sugar	300 mL
1 cup	corn syrup	250 mL
1 tsp	pure vanilla extract	5 mL
1/3 cup	unsalted butter, melted	75 mL

1. Preheat oven to 425° F (220° C). Roll out dough into a large rectangle to fit a standard jelly roll pan. Fit pastry into pan and crimp edges. Cover with pecans.

2. Beat eggs. Beat in sugar, corn syrup, vanilla and butter. Pour egg mixture over pecans.

3. Bake for 5 minutes. Reduce heat to 375° F (190° C) and bake for 15 to 20 minutes longer, or until filling is set. Cool.

Free-form Plum Tart

YIELD: Serves 8 to 10

*E*VERY *year when Jacques Pépin comes to teach at my cooking school, he prepares many delicious recipes. But, for some reason, there is always one recipe that stands out for me that I have to make right away and then over and over again. This is based on one of those.*

Now that I have children, whenever I cook at home I have help — whether I want it or not. When I made this recipe I explained to Mark and Anna (then four and two) that we were going to make plum tarts. They were very excited. I gave them some dough to roll out, and I had a big bowl of halved, pitted plums as well. I was making a large tart and they were making little ones. As I busily worked on mine, I didn't notice that they had reached for the whole plums in the fruit bowl. When I turned to inspect their work I saw two adorable tiny tarts with one big plum standing up on each! I sent a photograph to Jacques so that he could see how his recipes were being interpreted! (Their tarts were delicious, though, pits and all.)

1	recipe Sweet "Cookie" Pastry (page 86)	1
1/2 cup	finely chopped almonds	125 mL
3/4 cup	granulated sugar, divided	175 mL
1/4 cup	all-purpose flour	50 mL
1-1/2 lb	prune plums, halved and pitted	750 g
2 tbsp	unsalted butter	25 mL
1/2 cup	apricot jelly	125 mL

1. Preheat oven to 400° F (200° C).

2. Roll pastry into a rectangle approximately 16 × 12 inches (40 × 30 cm). Place on cookie sheet or upside-down baking sheet.

3. Combine nuts, 1/4 cup (50 mL) sugar and flour.

4. Sprinkle nut mixture over pastry to within 1 inch (2.5 cm) of border.

5. Place plums, cut side up, over nuts. Fold up pastry to make a border 1/2 inch (1 cm) high around plums. Pleat pastry slightly to fit. Patch breaks in pastry so juices will not leak out. Sprinkle tart with remaining sugar and dot with butter.

6. Bake for 40 to 50 minutes, or until fruit is tender and pastry is browned. Heat jelly, adding a little water if necessary and brush over the fruit.

Pear Cream Cheese Tart

*T*HIS *is so easy to make, but tastes so good. The crust is actually shortbread that you don't even have to roll out — you just pat it into the pan! This is delicious served warm or cold.*

YIELD: Serves 6 to 8

	Base	
1/2 cup	unsalted butter	125 mL
1/3 cup	granulated sugar	75 mL
1 cup	all-purpose flour	250 mL
	Filling	
2	ripe pears, preferably Bartlett	2
4 oz	cream cheese	125 g
1/2 cup	granulated sugar	125 mL
2	eggs	2
3/4 cup	light cream	175 mL
1/2 tsp	pure vanilla extract	2 mL
1/4 cup	sliced almonds	50 mL

1. Preheat oven to 425° F (220° C). Butter a 9 or 10 inch (23 or 25 cm) pie plate.

2. For the shortbread base, cream butter and sugar together until light. Beat in flour. Pat into pie plate.

3. Peel, halve and core pears. Slice. Arrange in circular rows on top of base.

4. Cream cheese until smooth. Beat in sugar. Add eggs one at a time, beating mixture smooth after each addition. Add cream and vanilla. Pour over pears. Sprinkle with almonds. (If there is any leftover custard, bake separately with any leftover pears or other fruit for a little treat for the chef.)

5. Bake for 10 minutes. Reduce heat to 375° F (190° C) and bake for 25 to 30 minutes longer, or until fruit is tender.

A Lighter Side: Use solid curd pressed cottage cheese instead of the cream cheese; use milk instead of cream.

Lemon and Orange Soufflé Tart

YIELD: Serves 8 to 10

THIS is a different and deliciously light version of a lemon meringue pie. The meringue is folded into the filling and baked. This causes the filling to puff like a soufflé into a light, fluffy texture. I like this at room temperature, but it is also good cold.

1	recipe Rich Pastry (page 86)	1
2 tbsp	orange marmalade	25 mL
4	eggs, separated	4
1/3 cup	granulated sugar	75 mL
2/3 cup	lemon juice	150 mL
2 tbsp	frozen orange juice concentrate	25 mL
1 tsp	finely grated orange peel	5 mL
1 tsp	finely grated lemon peel	5 mL
1/4 cup	unsalted butter	50 mL
1/2 cup	granulated sugar	125 mL
	Sifted icing sugar	

1. Preheat oven to 425° F (220° C).

2. Roll out dough into approximately 15 inch (38 cm) circle. Fit into a 10 inch (25 cm) flan pan with a removable bottom. Trim pastry but leave enough on the edge so that you can double edge of crust. Line with parchment paper or tin foil and fill with dried beans or pie weights. Bake for 15 minutes. Remove weights and paper. Reduce heat to 375° F (190° C). Bake for 10 minutes longer. Cool. Spread bottom with marmalade.

3. Meanwhile, beat egg yolks with 1/3 cup (75 mL) granulated sugar until very light and lemony in color. Beat in juices and peel. Transfer to a heavy saucepan and add butter. Cook over low heat until thickened. Remove from heat, transfer to a bowl, cover with buttered plastic wrap or waxed paper and cool.

4. In separate bowl, beat egg whites until light. Gradually beat in 1/2 cup (125 mL) granulated sugar and beat until firm. Fold into lemon base.

5. Spoon into prepared pie shell. Bake for 15 to 20 minutes, or until puffed and golden. Cool. Dust top with icing sugar.

Raspberry Hearts

THE look and flavor of this dessert make it seem hard to prepare. But the pastry is the only thing you have to make.

YIELD: Serves 8

1	recipe Quick Puff Pastry (page 87)	1
1	egg	1
1 tbsp	cream	15 mL
2 tbsp	granulated sugar	25 mL
2 cups	fresh raspberries	500 mL
2 cups	good-quality vanilla ice cream, melted	500 mL
2 tbsp	orange or raspberry liqueur	25 mL
1 cup	melted raspberry sorbet, homemade or commercial, or Raspberry Sauce (page 179)	250 mL
	Sifted icing sugar	

1. Preheat oven to 400° F (200° C). Line two baking sheets with parchment paper.

2. Roll out puff pastry to a thickness of 1/4 inch (5 mm). Cut out 8 to 10 6 x 4 inch (15 x 10 cm) hearts (make a pattern out of parchment paper and make more hearts than you need so that you can choose the nicest eight). Reroll scraps and freeze to use for pastry another time. Place hearts on baking sheets.

3. With the tip of a knife or a slightly smaller cookie cutter, trace a smaller heart about 1/2 inch (1 cm) in from the edge of each pastry heart. Do not go too deep into the pastry. Combine egg with cream. Brush on the hearts. Sprinkle with granulated sugar.

4. Bake for 25 to 30 minutes, or until golden-brown and puffed. Cool.

5. With your finger or the back of a spoon, press pastry down to indent the inner heart. Be gentle.

6. Fill indentation with raspberries.

7. Stir ice cream together with liqueur.

8. To serve, spoon approximately 1/4 cup (50 mL) ice cream sauce on each dessert plate. Place dots of raspberry sauce around inside edge of ice cream sauce. With the tip of a knife, join the dots in one continuous line (see page 31). Place a filled pastry heart in the center of each plate and dust everything with icing sugar.

Apple Custard Tart

*T*HIS is a creamy, custardy apple tart — probably my favorite. I love to use Spy apples for cooking as they are not too moist but have a wonderful strong, apple taste. Although Golden Delicious apples are not my favorite for eating, they do bake up nicely and are always available. Of course, if you have local apples that you love to bake with, use them.

1/2	recipe All-purpose Pastry (page 85)	1/2
1-1/4 cups	milk	300 mL
3	egg yolks	3
1/3 cup	granulated sugar	75 mL
2 tbsp	all-purpose flour	25 mL
1 tsp	pure vanilla extract	5 mL
2	apples, preferably Spy	2
1/2 cup	apricot jam	125 mL
1 tbsp	dark rum or orange liqueur	15 mL

1. Preheat oven to 425° F (220° C).

2. Roll out pastry to a thickness of 1/8 inch (3 mm) and fit into the bottom of a 10 inch (25 cm) quiche pan or tart pan. Line pastry with parchment paper and fill with pie weights or dried legumes. Bake for 15 minutes. Carefully remove weights and then paper. Cool for 10 minutes. Reduce oven temperature to 400° F (200° C).

3. Meanwhile, heat milk in a medium saucepan.

4. In bowl, beat egg yolks with sugar until light and lemony. Beat in flour. Whisk in hot milk and return mixture to saucepan. Cook on gentle heat, stirring constantly, until mixture comes to a boil and thickens. Remove from heat and stir in vanilla. Cool completely, stirring occasionally to prevent a skin from forming.

5. Peel apples. Halve and remove cores (a melon baller works very well for this). Slice apples thinly.

6. Spread cooled pastry cream in partially baked shell. Arrange apple slices in a circular pattern over the cream.

7. Bake for 30 to 35 minutes, or until fruit is tender.

8. Heat apricot jam with rum and stir until smooth. Brush apples with jam. Serve cold or at room temperature.

4

Cookies
and Other Sweets

ALTHOUGH many cooks are intimidated by baking cakes or handling pastry, people are rarely afraid of making cookies. Cookies seem to inspire confidence, so they are a natural place for beginners and children to start.

Cookies can be an after-school snack (Peanut Butter Chocolate Chunk, page 108), or they can be elegant and fancy (Lemon Coconut, page 112). They can be served as a wonderful rich dessert (Double Chocolate Brownies, page 120) or be made for an easy hostess gift (Hazelnut Biscotti, page 114).

Other delectables in this chapter include homemade truffles, which will spoil you forever for the storebought variety. The cookie and chocolate cups make delicious dessert containers and, to make your nibbling life complete, try the chocolate-dipped strawberries.

Cookie Tips

• Because cookies tend to be small and usually have short baking times, variances in oven temperatures can make a big difference in the results. Preheat your oven for at least 20 minutes before baking your first batch of cookies. As the oven preheats, the temperature sometimes fluctuates. Waiting 20 minutes before beginning to bake cookies should at least ensure that the oven will have settled at your desired temperature.

• Always use unsalted butter for greasing baking sheets, as it burns less easily. I definitely prefer the flavor of butter on the bottom of my cookies. If the cookies tend to stick, flour the baking sheets lightly after buttering them, but shake off any excess. Or line the sheets with non-stick parchment paper (see page 13). Grease the baking sheets around the edges so that the parchment stays in place. The parchment paper does not usually have to be buttered, and can be reused if you wipe it clean after each use.

• I like to use baking sheets with a little rim around the edge for cookies, since they prevent cookies or butter from dripping off the edge. If you prefer a flat edge or are making cookies that are hard to remove with a spatula, simply turn the baking sheet upside down and use it that way.

• Always set your timer for a minute or two less than the recipe suggests. For cookies, this is often one-quarter the baking time. This habit just ensures that if your oven is hotter than the oven of the recipe writer, your cookies will not burn. Cookies cook so quickly that a minute or two makes a big difference.

• Wait for about two minutes before removing cookies from the baking sheet. Cool cookies on wire racks that allow air to circulate so that the cookies do not get soggy. If you leave the cookies on the baking sheet too long and they stick, just return them to a hot oven for 30 to 60 seconds and try again.

• If you are making the cookies smaller than the recipe suggests, be sure to lessen the cooking time. Theoretically if the cookies are the same thickness they should take the same amount of time to cook, but sometimes this is not true. Protect yourself.

• If you want to know if a chewy cookie is done, remove one from the baking sheet and place in the refrigerator to cool quickly. If it firms up the way you wish, remove the others from the oven quickly. You have to underbake chewy cookies, but sometimes a minute can make the difference between uncooked and overbaked. If you consistently overbake your cookies, lower the oven temperature 25 degrees and try again.

• If you have a chocolate chip cookie recipe that you like but would prefer chewier cookies, reduce the flour by about 1/4 cup

(50 mL). If the batter is too creamy to shape into balls, refrigerate it for 30 minutes first, and reduce the cooking time by one or two minutes. If you prefer crisper cookies, add a little flour and bake a little longer.

• If you want to roll and cut cookies that you normally drop onto the baking sheet, simply add a little more flour until the dough can just be rolled. Do the opposite if you want to make drop cookies out of rolled cookies.

Molly's Squares

*F*OR *my CKFM radio spot last September, I was trying to dream up some wonderful lunch box cookie to feature on the show. Marie Jones, who was the manager of the cooking school, said her mother-in-law, Molly Haldenby, used to make these sensational cookies for her children. When we tested the recipe we tried to save some to take to the radio station for treats, but, alas, we ate them all. I hope you have better luck getting them to your lunch box!*

YIELD:
Approximately 36 small squares

1/2 cup	peanut butter	125 mL
1/2 cup	brown sugar	125 mL
1/2 cup	corn syrup	125 mL
2 tbsp	unsalted butter	25 mL
1-1/2 cups	Rice Krispies	375 mL
1/2 cup	Special K	125 mL
3/4 cup	chopped peanuts	175 mL
	Topping	
4 oz	bittersweet or semisweet chocolate, chopped	125 g
3 tbsp	unsalted butter	50 mL

1. Place peanut butter, brown sugar and corn syrup in a saucepan. Cook until bubbly and well combined.

2. Stir in butter, Rice Krispies, Special K and peanuts.

3. Press mixture into an 8 inch (2 L) square baking dish.

4. Melt chocolate with butter in the top of a double boiler over gently simmering water. Spread over cookie mixture. Refrigerate until firm. Cut into squares.

A **Lighter Side:** Do not ice cookies; omit peanuts.

Chunky Chocolate Chip Cookies

*T*HIS *is a traditional chocolate chip cookie, except that the chocolate chips are large chunks of delicious European chocolate, both dark and white.*

One neat trick for making children's cookies is to use tiny pieces of chocolate and make the cookies the size of quarters. Bake for about half the normal cooking time.

1 cup	unsalted butter	250 mL
1 cup	brown sugar	250 mL
1/4 cup	granulated sugar	50 mL
1	egg	1
1 tsp	pure vanilla extract	5 mL
2 cups	all-purpose flour	500 mL
1/4 tsp	salt	1 mL
1 tsp	baking soda	5 mL
3 oz	bittersweet or semisweet chocolate, cut into 1/4 inch (5 mm) chunks	90 g
3 oz	white chocolate, cut into 1/4 inch (5 mm) chunks	90 g
1/2 cup	toasted pecans, cut into 1/4 inch (5 mm) pieces	125 mL

1. In large bowl, cream butter with sugars until light. Add egg and vanilla and beat well.

2. In separate bowl, sift flour with salt and baking soda and add to batter. Stir in just until batter comes together. Stir in chocolates and nuts.

3. Refrigerate batter for 1 hour.

4. Preheat over to 375° F (190° C). Line baking sheets with parchment paper, or butter and flour lightly.

5. Shape cookies into 1-1/2 inch (4 cm) balls and arrange on cookie sheets about 2 inches (5 cm) apart. Flatten well.

6. Bake for 8 to 10 minutes. The longer they bake, the crisper they will be.

A **Lighter Side:** Use half the amount of chocolate and nuts. Make the cookies a little smaller (but don't eat more!).

Chocolate Chunk Shortbreads

*T*HESE *cookies combine my all-time favorite shortbread recipe with the popular idea of having large chunks of chocolate and nuts in cookies. Fruit sugar, also called "berry," "bar," "castor," or "instant dissolving," is finely ground granulated sugar that can be purchased or made by processing sugar in a blender or food processor for 30 seconds. Measure after processing.*

YIELD:
Approximately 60 cookies

2 cups	salted butter, at room temperature	500 mL
1 cup	fruit sugar	250 mL
3-1/2 cups	all-purpose flour	875 mL
1/2 cup	rice flour	125 mL
8 oz	bittersweet or semisweet chocolate, cut into 1/2 inch (1 cm) chunks	250 g
1 cup	pecans, toasted and cut into 1/2 inch (1 cm) chunks	250 mL
1/3 cup	sifted icing sugar, approx.	75 mL

1. Preheat oven to 350° F (180° C). Line baking sheets with parchment paper, or butter and flour lightly.

2. In large bowl, cream butter with sugar until very light.

3. In a separate bowl, stir or sift all-purpose flour with rice flour. Beat into butter mixture.

4. Stir in chocolate and pecans.

5. Mound batter in tablespoon-sized amounts onto baking sheets, about 1 inch (2.5 cm) apart.

6. Bake for 20 to 25 minutes, or until ever so lightly browned. Cool on wire racks.

7. When cookies are cool, dust lightly with icing sugar.

A **Lighter Side:** Use half the amount of chocolate and nuts.

Peanut Butter Chocolate Chunk Cookies

YIELD:
Approximately 40 cookies

*I*F *you love peanuts and chocolate, this is your cookie. For a great sundae, chop up the cookies, sprinkle over vanilla ice cream and serve with chocolate sauce.*

1/2 cup	unsalted butter	125 mL
1/2 cup	peanut butter (smooth or chunky)	125 mL
1/2 cup	brown sugar	125 mL
1/2 cup	granulated sugar	125 mL
1	egg	1
1 tsp	pure vanilla extract	5 mL
1-1/2 cups	all-purpose flour	375 mL
1/2 tsp	baking soda	2 mL
pinch	salt	pinch
1/3 cup	coarsely chopped peanuts	75 mL
4 oz	bittersweet or semisweet chocolate, cut into 1/2 inch (1 cm) chunks	125 g

1. Preheat oven to 350° F (180° C). Butter two baking sheets or line with parchment paper.

2. In large bowl, cream butter with peanut butter. Beat in sugars. Add egg and vanilla.

3. In separate bowl, combine or sift together flour, baking soda and salt. Stir into butter mixture. Mix in peanuts and chocolate. Knead a little if necessary to bring dough together.

4. Shape dough into 1-1/2 inch (4 cm) balls. Arrange on prepared baking sheets about 1 inch (2.5 cm) apart. Flatten cookies slightly.

5. Bake for 12 to 15 minutes, or until crisp. (If you like chewier cookies, bake them for 12 minutes.) Cool on racks.

A Lighter Side: Omit the chopped peanuts. Chop the chocolate into smaller pieces, and use half the amount.

Painted Sugar Cookies

*E*VERY *year I invite my children's nursery or kindergarten class to my school for a special cooking lesson. One year I baked and iced many shapes of these cookies and then let the children paint them. I made three different colors of "paint" and provided lots of little paintbrushes. The results were stunning, and the children got to take their artwork home (though most of them chose to eat it!).*

I like to use paste food colorings in icings and playdough, as the colors are very vibrant. By the way, cookie decorating is also a terrific activity for kids' birthday parties. Put the recipe and the cookies in their loot bags!

YIELD:
Approximately 50 cookies

1 cup	unsalted butter	250 mL
1 cup	granulated sugar	250 mL
1	egg	1
1 tsp	pure vanilla extract	5 mL
2 cups	all-purpose flour	500 mL
1/2 tsp	baking powder	2 mL
pinch	salt	pinch
	Icing and Paint	
2 cups	sifted icing sugar	500 mL
1/4 cup	water	50 mL
	Food coloring	

1. In large bowl, cream butter until light. Beat in sugar gradually. Beat in egg and vanilla.

2. In separate bowl, sift flour with baking powder and salt. Beat into butter mixture, stirring only until combined. Refrigerate dough for 1 hour.

3. Preheat oven to 375° F (190° C). Line baking sheets with parchment paper.

4. Divide dough into four pieces. Roll out each piece to 1/4 inch (5 mm) thickness. Cut into shapes and place on baking sheet.

5. Bake for 8 to 10 minutes, or until just beginning to color. Cool on racks.

6. Combine icing sugar with water. Brush a thin coating of icing over cookies. Allow to dry for 10 minutes.

7. Divide remaining icing into four small containers. (You should have enough, but make more icing if you have iced the cookies extra thick!) Add a different food coloring to each pot. Thin with a little water if necessary. Using a small paintbrush, paint each cookie as you wish. Allow to dry.

Gwen's Caramel Slices

YIELD:
Approximately 64
cookies

*T*HIS *recipe looks so short and easy that I may have overlooked it if Gwen Fargeon hadn't been the person who gave it to me. Gwen is one of the very best cooks I know, and anything she raves about has to be great! My cousin Barbara Glickman also makes these all the time — with pecans.*

1 cup	unsalted butter	250 mL
1 cup	packed brown sugar	250 mL
32	Graham crackers	32
1 cup	sliced almonds	250 mL

1. Preheat oven to 350° F (180° C). Line a large baking sheet with foil.

2. Place butter and sugar in a saucepan and cook, stirring, until mixture is smooth. Boil for 2 minutes.

3. Arrange crackers on cookie sheet, overlapping them just a tiny bit.

4. Pour butter/sugar mixture over top as evenly as possible.

5. Sprinkle with almonds.

6. Bake for 10 to 12 minutes — cookies will look saucy but will harden as they cool. Cool on cookie sheet. Cut each cracker into two pieces.

Ladyfingers

YIELD:
Approximately 32
ladyfingers

*W*HEN *making ladyfingers, it is always worth making a lot. They can be used in so many ways and freeze beautifully. Although special baking pans for ladyfingers are available and certainly are elegant, I find it easier just to use a piping tube with a plain nozzle to shape them.*

6	eggs, separated	6
1 cup	fruit sugar, divided	250 mL
1 tsp	pure vanilla extract	5 mL
1-1/3 cups	all-purpose flour	325 mL
1/2 cup	sifted icing sugar	125 mL

1. Preheat oven to 325° F (160° C). Butter and flour three baking sheets, or line with parchment paper.

2. In large bowl, whisk egg yolks with 1/2 cup (125 mL) fruit sugar and vanilla.

3. In separate bowl, beat egg whites until light. Slowly add remaining 1/2 cup (125 mL) fruit sugar and beat until stiff. Fold whites into yolks.

4. Sift flour over mixture and fold in lightly but thoroughly.

5. Transfer mixture into a pastry bag with a plain 3/4 inch (2 cm) nozzle and pipe batter onto baking sheets in 4 × 1 inch (10 × 2.5 cm) strips, about 2 inches (5 cm) apart. Sift icing sugar over the cookies.

6. Bake for 12 to 15 minutes, or until firm but still pale. Allow to rest for 15 minutes, and then remove from baking sheet. Store in a covered container.

Orange Pecan Cookies

*O*RANGES *and pecans are a delicious combination. These cookies are perfect for a sophisticated tea party.*

YIELD:
Approximately 50 cookies

1 cup	unsalted butter	250 mL
1 cup	brown sugar	250 mL
2	egg yolks	2
2 tsp	finely grated orange peel	10 mL
1 tsp	pure vanilla extract	5 mL
2 cups	all-purpose flour	500 mL
2/3 cup	toasted pecans, finely chopped	150 mL
2 tbsp	fresh orange juice	25 mL
3/4 cup	sifted icing sugar, approx.	175 mL

1. In large bowl, cream butter with brown sugar until light. Beat in egg yolks, orange peel and vanilla.

2. In separate bowl, combine flour with pecans and stir into butter mixture only until blended. Refrigerate dough for 30 minutes.

3. Preheat oven to 350° F (180° C). Line two or three baking sheets with parchment paper or butter and flour lightly.

4. Shape cookies into 1-1/2 inch (4 cm) balls and place on baking sheets about 1 inch (2.5 cm) apart. Press cookies flat with the bottom of a glass dipped in flour.

5. Bake for 10 to 12 minutes, or until cookies just begin to color. Cool on wire racks.

6. Combine orange juice with enough icing sugar to form a glaze. Glaze should be slightly runny. Brush on top of cooled cookies and allow to set.

Lemon Coconut Cookies

YIELD:
Approximately 30 cookies

S INCE Linda Stephen, my associate teacher at the cooking school, returned from her culinary tour of Southeast Asia, I've been reintroduced to the wonderful flavor of coconut. I really like it in these delicate, thin little cookies. If you prefer a stronger coconut flavor, toast the grated coconut lightly before using.

1/2 cup	unsalted butter	125 mL
1/4 cup	granulated sugar	50 mL
1 tsp	pure vanilla extract	5 mL
1 tsp	finely grated lemon peel	5 mL
1 cup	cake and pastry flour, sifted	250 mL
1/2 cup	grated unsweetened coconut	125 mL
	Glaze	
1/2 cup	sifted icing sugar	125 mL
2 tbsp	lemon juice	25 mL
2 tbsp	grated unsweetened coconut	25 mL

1. In large bowl, cream butter until light. Beat in granulated sugar gradually. Add vanilla and peel.

2. Stir in flour just until blended. Add coconut. If dough is too soft to handle, refrigerate for 30 minutes.

3. Preheat oven to 300° F (150° C). Line a baking sheet with parchment paper or butter and flour lightly.

4. Shape dough into 1-1/2 inch (4 cm) balls. Place on baking sheet about 1 inch (2.5 cm) apart. Flatten balls with the bottom of a glass dipped in sugar.

5. Bake for 20 to 25 minutes, or until cookies just begin to turn golden. Cool cookies on racks.

6. Combine icing sugar with lemon juice. Mixture should be runny. Brush on cookies and sprinkle with a little coconut.

Turtle Squares

*T*HESE *squares were my testers' favorite. They include everything I love that's sweet — caramel, chocolate and shortbread. The caramel is slightly runny, so the cookies are best stored in the refrigerator or freezer and served cold.*

YIELD:
Approximately 60 cookies

	Shortbread	
1 cup	unsalted butter	250 mL
3/4 cup	brown sugar	175 mL
2 cups	all-purpose flour	500 mL
	Caramel	
1-2/3 cups	brown sugar	400 mL
1 cup	whipping cream	250 mL
1 cup	corn syrup	250 mL
1/2 cup	unsalted butter	125 mL
1 tsp	pure vanilla extract	5 mL
2 cups	chopped toasted pecans	500 mL
	Topping	
8 oz	bittersweet or semisweet chocolate	250 g
1/3 cup	whipping cream	75 mL
2 tbsp	unsalted butter	25 mL
1 cup	pecan halves	250 mL

1. Preheat oven to 350° F (180° C). Butter a jelly roll pan.

2. To make shortbread, cream butter and sugar in large bowl. Beat in flour. Press mixture as evenly as possible into bottom of pan.

3. Bake shortbread for 15 to 18 minutes.

4. Meanwhile, to prepare caramel, place brown sugar, cream, corn syrup and butter in a medium saucepan. Bring to a boil and cook for about 5 minutes, to soft ball stage — 234° F (112° C). Stir in vanilla and chopped pecans. Pour caramel over base. Cool.

6. To make icing, cut chocolate into small pieces and place in a bowl with cream and butter. Place over simmering water and stir until mixture is melted and smooth. Spread over caramel.

7. Allow chocolate icing to set before cutting cookies into squares. Place one pecan on each cookie.

Hazelnut Biscotti or Mandel Broidt

YIELD:
Approximately 36
cookies

I'VE often thought it would be fun to follow a recipe around the world and see whom it meets and how it changes from each encounter. Biscotti are Italian dunking cookies that are all the rage right now. How could I have grown up with them in a Jewish household? We called them mandel broidt or "almond bread," although they often contain nuts other than almonds and do not really resemble bread. They are baked twice to give them their characteristic crunch and dryness — once in loaves, and then sliced into individual cookies. For a fancy presentation, pipe squiggles of melted chocolate on their sides as shown.

1/2 cup	unsalted butter	125 mL
1/2 cup	vegetable oil, preferably safflower	125 mL
1 cup	granulated sugar	250 mL
3	eggs	3
2 tbsp	finely grated orange peel	25 mL
1 tbsp	frozen orange juice concentrate, thawed	15 mL
1 tsp	pure vanilla extract	5 mL
3 cups	all-purpose flour	750 mL
2 tsp	baking powder	10 mL
pinch	salt	pinch
1-1/2 cups	toasted hazelnuts, coarsely chopped	375 mL
4 oz	bittersweet or semisweet chocolate, melted, optional	125 g

1. Preheat oven to 350° F (180° C). Line two baking sheets with parchment paper, or butter and flour lightly.

2. In large bowl, cream butter until light. Gradually beat in oil. Add sugar, beating constantly. Add eggs one at a time, beating well after each addition. Add orange peel, orange juice concentrate and vanilla.

3. Sift or mix flour with baking powder and salt. Mix into batter. Add nuts. Knead well until a manageable dough is formed.

4. Divide dough into three pieces. Shape each piece into a loaf that is about 1-1/2 inches (4 cm) high and 3 inches (8 cm) wide. Place on baking sheets.

5. Bake loaves for 25 to 30 minutes, or until somewhat firm. Remove from oven and lower oven temperature to 300° F (150° C).

6. Gently slice loaves into 1/2 inch (1 cm) slices. Arrange flat on baking sheets. Bake for 25 to 30 minutes longer, or until cookies are firm and dry. Turn cookies over partway through baking. Cool on racks.

7. If you are using chocolate, place melted chocolate in a piping tube or clean plastic squeeze bottle. Pipe a squiggle down one side. Allow to dry until set before serving.

Hazelnut Praline

*F*OR a caramel addict like me, this is one of the most delicious treats. It is more like a candy than a cookie and is usually chopped and used as a topping for ice cream, or ground and used in a mousse or whipped cream mixture. I drizzle melted chocolate all over it, cut it into chunks and eat it. You can store praline in the refrigerator for one month, or longer in the freezer. It is also good when made with almonds (or sometimes I combine almonds with hazelnuts).

YIELD:
Approximately
2 cups (500 mL)

1 cup	granulated sugar	250 mL
3 tbsp	cold water	50 mL
1-1/2 cups	hazelnuts, toasted	375 mL

1. Place sugar with water in a heavy saucepan. Cook over medium or medium-high heat, stirring, until sugar dissolves.

2. Stop stirring and cook until sugar turns a golden caramel color. Brush down sides of saucepan occasionally with a pastry brush dipped in cold water. (If mixture crystallizes, you can add a little more water and continue cooking until mixture is smooth again, but I usually start over. Remember, once sugar has dissolved, don't stir!)

3. When sugar is caramel colored, stir in nuts.

4. Spread mixture out on buttered baking sheet and allow to cool for 1 hour.

5. Break praline up with a knife, chop or pulverize in a food processor.

Apricot Almond Rugulahs

YIELD:
Approximately 24
cookies

*T*HIS *cream cheese pastry is one of the most delicious, and one of the easiest to handle. You can also use it for fruit tarts and quiches. The pastry can be made by hand or in a food processor.*

These crescent cookies freeze very well baked or unbaked. Bake them from the frozen state — they will just take a few minutes longer to cook.

	Cream Cheese Pastry	
1 cup	all-purpose flour	250 mL
1/2 cup	unsalted butter, cold	125 mL
4 oz	cream cheese, cold	125 g
	Filling	
3/4 cup	apricot jam	175 mL
1/4 cup	granulated sugar	50 mL
1/2 cup	chopped toasted almonds	125 mL
1 tsp	finely grated lemon peel	5 mL
	Topping	
1	egg	1
1/3 cup	coarse granulated sugar or chopped almonds	75 mL
	Sifted icing sugar	

1. To make pastry, place flour in bowl. Cut butter into small pieces and rub into flour with your fingers or a pastry blender. Cut cheese into small cubes and rub into flour-butter mixture. Knead until dough forms a ball.

2. Cut dough in half, wrap each half in plastic wrap and refrigerate.

3. To make filling, stir jam until it is spreadable.

4. In bowl, combine sugar with nuts and peel.

5. On a floured surface, roll out each piece of dough. The larger and thinner the circle, the crisper the cookies will be. Each circle should be at least 9 inches (23 cm) in diameter. Spread each circle with jam and sprinkle with almond mixture.

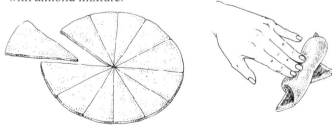

6. Cut each circle into twelve wedges. Roll up each wedge tightly from the outside edge. Turn edges in slightly to form a crescent. Place on a parchment paper-lined baking sheet about 1 inch (2.5 cm) apart. Repeat until all cookies are shaped.

7. Preheat oven to 350° F (180° C).

8. Beat egg and brush cookies with beaten egg. Sprinkle with coarse sugar or nuts.

9. Bake cookies for 20 to 25 minutes, or until golden. Cool on racks. Dust with sifted icing sugar.

A Lighter Side: Use solid curd pressed cottage cheese instead of cream cheese. Omit sugar, nuts and lemon peel in filling — just use jam.

Candied Orange Peel

*W*HEN *removing the peel from the oranges, I like to include the white pithy part under the peel. It becomes tender and less bitter when fully cooked (although some people prefer the peel without the pith).*

YIELD:
Approximately 48 pieces

6	thick-skinned oranges	6
	Water	
6 cups	granulated sugar, divided	1.5 L

1. With a sharp knife, remove peel from oranges (include the white part beneath the peel if you wish). You should get at least eight large pieces of peel from each orange. Place peel in a large pot of water and bring to a boil. Cook for 15 minutes on medium heat. Drain and repeat procedure.

2. Combine 1-1/2 cups (375 mL) sugar in a large pot with 8 cups (2 L) water. Bring to a boil. Add peel. Cook on medium-high heat for 30 to 45 minutes, or until peel is tender and syrup has almost been completely absorbed. Drain.

3. Place remaining sugar on a flat baking sheet. Working with a few pieces of peel at a time, dredge with sugar and then allow to dry on racks set over baking sheets or waxed paper. Allow peel to dry overnight.

Thumbprint Cookies

YIELD:
Approximately 50 cookies

*T*HESE *are a cross between shortbread cookies and tiny jam tarts. They are much easier to make than tarts, but look as pretty and fanciful with the different-colored jams shimmering in the center. I have been making these for years and have noticed how they have changed with the different kinds of jams and jellies that are in vogue. One of my favorites now is the Scotch orange marmalade!*

My children won't eat these cookies, because they don't like jam or nuts, but they love to make the holes!

1 cup	unsalted butter	250 mL
1/3 cup	light brown sugar	75 mL
1/3 cup	granulated sugar	75 mL
2	egg yolks	2
1 tsp	pure vanilla extract	5 mL
2-1/4 cups	all-purpose flour	550 mL
pinch	salt	pinch
2	egg whites	2
1-1/2 cups	finely chopped pecans, hazelnuts or almonds	375 mL
1 cup	assorted jams or jellies, approx.	250 mL

1. Preheat oven to 350° F (180° C). Butter and lightly flour baking sheets or line with parchment paper.

2. Cream butter until light. Beat in brown and granulated sugars. Add egg yolks and vanilla and beat until well blended.

3. Combine flour with salt and add to batter. Stir just until dough is formed.

4. Shape cookies into 1 inch (2.5 cm) balls, place on a tray and refrigerate while assembling other ingredients.

5. Lightly beat egg white in a shallow bowl. Place finely chopped nuts in another shallow dish.

6. Roll each ball of cookie dough in egg white and then lightly in nuts. Place on prepared pans about 1 inch (2.5 cm) apart. Press center of each cookie in slightly to make an indentation for the jam.

7. Bake for 9 to 12 minutes, or until cookies are lightly browned. If centers have risen slightly, gently press indentation again. Cool on racks.

8. When cookies are cool, spoon a little jam or jelly into the centers.

Chocolate Brownie Cookies

*T*HESE *cookies are so moist and chewy, they remind me of a brownie. They freeze well and actually taste delicious frozen as they melt in your mouth. If you cannot find really fresh walnuts, use pecans. If the nuts are toasted first (see page 20), they will add a richer taste to the cookies. You can leave out the marshmallows, but they do add a wonderful chewiness.*

YIELD:
Approximately 36 large cookies

1 lb	bittersweet or semisweet chocolate, chopped	500 g
1/4 cup	unsalted butter	50 mL
1 cup	miniature white marshmallows	250 mL
1/2 cup	all-purpose flour	125 mL
1/2 tsp	baking powder	2 mL
1/4 tsp	salt	1 mL
4	eggs	4
1-1/2 cups	granulated sugar	375 mL
10 oz	bittersweet or semisweet chocolate, chopped	300 g
2 cups	chopped toasted walnuts or pecans	500 mL

1. Preheat oven to 350° F (180° C). Melt 1 lb (500 g) chocolate and butter over barely simmering water. Cool slightly and then stir in marshmallows until partially melted. Reserve.

2. Sift together the flour, baking powder and salt. Reserve.

3. In large bowl, beat eggs with sugar until light and stir in melted chocolate. Add flour mixture, 10 oz (300 g) chopped chocolate and nuts. Refrigerate dough until it is cool enough to handle.

4. Shape dough into two fat rolls about 3 inches (7.5 cm) in diameter — like refrigerator cookies (you can make smaller cookies by making the rolls smaller in diameter). Roll in additional flour and wrap well in waxed paper. Freeze for at least 1 hour, or until firm.

5. Preheat oven to 350° F (180° C). Line baking sheets with parchment paper. Slice cookies 1/2 inch (1 cm) thick.

6. Place on baking sheets about 2 inches (5 cm) apart and bake for 10 to 12 minutes — just until they lose their sheen. They should just "set up" when cool and should be moist and sticky inside. Cool on racks

Lois's Double Chocolate Brownies

YIELD:
Approximately 36 to
40 squares

I have never found a better brownie than this one. Lois Lilienstein, of Sharon, Lois and Bram fame, gave me this recipe years ago. Besides being thankful for these brownies, I also want to thank the trio for inviting me on "The Elephant Show." Even though I only played myself, I really felt like I was making my movie debut! And I think I was even more excited than my children when I saw the show months later!

4 oz	unsweetened chocolate, chopped	125 g
6 oz	bittersweet or semisweet chocolate, chopped	175 g
1 cup	unsalted butter	250 mL
4	eggs	4
2 cups	granulated sugar	500 mL
2 tsp	pure vanilla extract	10 mL
1 cup	all-purpose flour	250 mL
1/2 tsp	salt	2 mL
1 tsp	baking powder	5 mL
2 cups	miniature white marshmallows	500 mL
3 oz	bittersweet or semisweet chocolate, chopped	90 g
1 cup	chopped toasted pecans or walnuts	250 mL
	Glaze	
4 oz	bittersweet or semisweet chocolate, chopped	125 g
1/4 cup	whipping cream	50 mL
40	toasted pecan or walnut halves	40

1. Preheat oven to 350° F (180° C). Butter a 13 × 9 inch (3.5 L) baking dish and line with parchment paper.

2. Combine unsweetened chocolate and 6 oz (175 g) bittersweet chocolate in the top of a double boiler over simmering water. Add butter. Stir until melted and smooth. Cool slightly.

3. In large bowl, beat eggs with sugar until light. Beat in vanilla and melted chocolate.

4. In separate bowl, mix or sift flour with salt and baking powder. Stir into batter just until blended. Stir in marshmallows and 3 oz (90 g) chopped chocolate. Pour batter into pan and sprinkle with chopped nuts.

5. Bake for 30 to 40 minutes, or just until top loses its sheen. Brownies will be quite soft when removed from oven but will firm up when cool. Cool completely and then chill.

6. Run a knife around the inside edge of pan and invert. Trim edges and eat them. Cut brownies into squares.

7. For the glaze, melt chocolate and cream. Stir until smooth. Ice each brownie and top with a pecan or walnut half. Refrigerate or freeze until ready to serve.

Chocolate Cups

*I*T is so easy to make your own chocolate cups. The first time you prepare them it will take a little longer, though, so give yourself enough time to get used to it. I use really good-quality chocolate and always buy more than the recipe specifies, so if I accidentally make the cups too thin and they break as I am peeling off the paper, I can melt more chocolate and recoat them without having to run out for more chocolate.

You can also make the cups with white chocolate or milk chocolate. If you use coating chocolate (see page 18), be sure to use the best that you can find. Coating chocolate will make the cups easier to handle, but bittersweet chocolate will give you a more intense, pure chocolate flavor.

YIELD:
Approximately 12 to 16 large cups or 24 small cups

1 lb	bittersweet or semisweet chocolate	500 g

1. Chop chocolate into small pieces. Place in a metal bowl set over simmering water just until melted. Stir to complete melting.

2. With a small spoon or pastry brush (I prefer a spoon), "paint" the inside of fluted paper cups. (Foil cups are easier to use than regular paper cups.) Place in a muffin tin for support and freeze for at least 30 minutes. If chocolate is too hot, it will just run down the sides and will not be thick enough to coat paper well. If this happens, just cool chocolate a little before continuing.

3. Working with one cup at a time (leave remaining cups in freezer), carefully peel off paper. Return cups to freezer. If cups tend to break when you peel off paper, melt a little more chocolate and coat the sides again, reinforcing the first coating (it's easier than remelting the cups and starting over). Cups can also be painted twice intentionally — dark chocolate first, with a second coating of white chocolate (see page 159).

Almond Cookie Cups or Cones

YIELD:
Approximately 16
large cups or cones

*T*HESE *thin almond wafers can easily be molded into cups or cones and then filled with ice cream, mousse or whipped cream. However, if they are filled too far in advance, the cookie will become soggy. When entertaining, it is wonderful to be able to prepare dessert ahead of time, so I usually line the cups or cones with melted chocolate. When it hardens it will protect the cookie from the moisture in the filling. And it's delicious, too!*

You can also serve Cappuccino Mousse (see page 161) in a cookie "cup and saucer." Leave one cookie flat and shape another into a little cup. Set the cup on the saucer, and fill the cup with mousse.

1/3 cup	all-purpose flour	75 mL
1/2 cup	granulated sugar	125 mL
2	egg whites	2
1/4 cup	unsalted butter, melted	50 mL
2 tsp	water	10 mL
1 tsp	pure vanilla extract	5 mL
1/4 tsp	pure almond extract	1 mL
1/4 cup	sliced almonds	50 mL
1 lb	bittersweet or semisweet chocolate (or good-quality coating chocolate)	500 g

1. Preheat oven to 375° F (190° C). Butter and flour cookie sheets or upside-down baking sheets. (It is easier to remove the cookies from rimless sheets.)

2. Mix together flour and sugar. Whisk in remaining ingredients except chocolate.

3. Use a spoonful of batter for each cookie and spread as thinly as possible. Bake only three at a time if you intend to shape them, as they cool quickly.

4. Bake for 3 to 5 minutes, or until slightly brown around the edges.

5. If you are making wafers, remove from baking sheet and let cookies cool flat. If you are making cones, remove from sheet and, while the cookie is hot, roll up with one end pinched and the rest flaring out to form a cone. For cups, mold hot cookie over an upside-down baking cup or small brioche mold. As soon as cookie is cold, it will retain its shape. To make cookie "tacos," mold over a small rolling pin or in taco molds. (If cookie becomes too cool to remove from baking sheet and shape, return pan to oven for 30 to 60 seconds.)

6. Chop chocolate and melt over gently simmering water, stirring until

smooth. Cool slightly. Spoon about 1/4 cup (50 mL) melted chocolate into each cup or cone and swirl it around until the chocolate coats the inside completely. Pour out any excess chocolate. Place on a rack to set. Cookies are quite thin and delicate, so be careful! Store shaped cookies in an airtight tin or freeze. If you are using a sauce, add it just before serving.

Grand Marnier Heart Truffles

NOT only are these truffles delicious to eat; they are fanciful to look at. Of course, you can cut them into any shape — moons, stars, diamonds — but hearts are my favorite.

YIELD:
Approximately 48 truffles

12 oz	bittersweet or semisweet chocolate, chopped	375 g
1/2 cup	unsalted butter	125 mL
2	egg yolks	2
2 tbsp	Grand Marnier or other orange liqueur	25 mL
1/2 cup	sifted cocoa or icing sugar	125 mL

1. Place bittersweet chocolate and butter in top of double boiler over gently simmering water. Cook, stirring constantly, until melted and smooth.

2. Beat in egg yolks. Cook gently, stirring, for 1 minute. Stir in liqueur.

3. Line a square 9 inch (2.5 L) baking dish with plastic wrap. Pour in chocolate mixture and spread as evenly as possible. Cover with another sheet of plastic wrap, smoothing out chocolate. Refrigerate for several hours or overnight.

4. Remove top sheet of plastic. Run a knife around edge of pan if necessary and lift out solid chocolate. With a 1 inch (2.5 cm) heart-shaped cookie cutter, cut out heart shapes, as close to each other as possible. (If mixture seems too brittle, leave chocolate at room temperature for 5 minutes and try again.) Shape leftover chocolate into small balls, as for regular truffles.

5. Dust hearts with sifted cocoa or icing sugar. Refrigerate or freeze.

Raspberry Truffles Dipped in Chocolate

YIELD:
Approximately 50 truffles

*T*HESE *are my favorite truffles. I like to make them small — approximately 3/4 inch (2 cm) in diameter (before dipping) so that you can eat them in one bite.*

You probably will not need the whole pound of chocolate for coating the truffles, but it is hard to work with less. The method described for coating the truffles is the one used by professional pastry chefs. It is a little messy but a lot of fun once you get used to it. If you prefer, you can always dip the truffles into a bowl of chocolate with a fork.

12 oz	bittersweet or semisweet chocolate	375 g
1/3 cup	whipping cream	75 mL
1/3 cup	unsalted butter	75 mL
1/3 cup	icing sugar	75 mL
1	egg yolk	1
1/4 cup	Chambord or other raspberry liqueur	50 mL
1 lb	bittersweet, semisweet or good-quality coating chocolate	500 g
1/2 cup	sifted cocoa	125 mL

1. Melt 12 oz (375 g) chocolate with cream and butter in a double boiler over gentle heat.

2. Stir in icing sugar and combine well. Beat in egg yolk. Cook for 2 minutes longer. Remove from heat and stir in liqueur.

3. Transfer chocolate mixture to a bowl or pan. Refrigerate overnight until firm.

4. Shape mixture into 48 to 60 little truffles. Arrange on a waxed paper-lined baking sheet and freeze or refrigerate until firm and very cold.

5. Melt 1 lb (500 g) chocolate over simmering water and pour into shallow pan. Have cocoa in a second shallow pan beside the chocolate. Have a second baking sheet ready for finished truffles (use little foil cups if desired).

6. Remove truffles from the refrigerator. Dip your (clean) hands palm side down into the warm chocolate. Roll each truffle in your chocolaty hands to coat well. Roll in cocoa. Place truffle in foil cup or on baking sheet. Repeat until all truffles are dipped and rolled in cocoa. Refrigerate or freeze. Refrigerate extra dipping chocolate for dipping strawberries (see page 126) or more truffles.

Chocolate Fondant "Pasta" Decorations

I call these pasta decorations because the easiest way to roll the dough is through a roller-style pasta machine. (You can roll it with a rolling pin, but it is quite a chore.) The results are miraculous. If you want a sheet of thin chocolate to wrap around a cake (see Chocolate Fantasy Cake on page 66); if you want chocolate fettuccine to decorate the top of a cake (see Coffee Hazelnut Dacquoise on page 46); or if you want to fashion large roses out of sheets of malleable chocolate to place in the center of a cake (see Bittersweet Chocolate Cheesecake on page 74), this is the way to do it! You can make these decorations with dark chocolate or white chocolate.

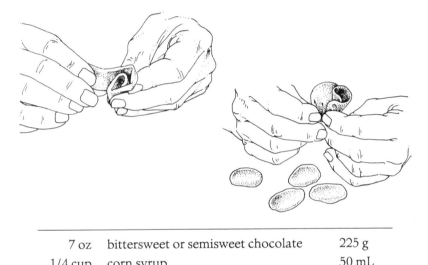

7 oz	bittersweet or semisweet chocolate	225 g
1/4 cup	corn syrup	50 mL

1. Melt chocolate over gently simmering water. Stir in corn syrup. Do not worry if mixture seizes up and appears strange.

2. Wrap in plastic wrap and refrigerate for about 1 hour.

3. Knead chocolate until smooth, wrap again and allow to rest for at least 1 hour at room temperature.

4. Divide mixture into four pieces. Using a hand-cranked pasta machine, set rollers at widest width. Press one piece of chocolate dough through. Fold into thirds and press through again. Repeat two or three times.

5. Set rollers one notch closer together and pass dough through only once. Set rollers one notch closer and repeat until chocolate is as thin as possible without breaking.

Chocolate-dipped Strawberries

YIELD: 16 large
strawberries

Y OU *can serve these for dessert, as a snack, along with or instead of truffles as a second dessert, or you can put them around a cake as an edible and gorgeous crown.*

Although these strawberries are very easy to make, there are a few tricks that will make them even easier. The berries should be dry when they are dipped into the chocolate. Some berries do not even need washing — wiping them with a damp cloth is enough. If they are sandy and need to be rinsed, be sure to dry them thoroughly, as a drop of water in the chocolate could cause the chocolate to seize (see page 30).

When dipping, if the greens are nice, dip the pointed end and use the greens as a handle for dipping. If the greens are not in good condition, hull the berries and dip the fat end.

Allow the berries to set on waxed paper-lined baking sheets. Refrigerate them for faster setting. The berries taste best when eaten on the same day; they will get a little moist if left sitting too long.

I like to use European bittersweet chocolate for dipping. Good-quality coating chocolate (see page 18) can also be used, and although the finished berries will look shinier and be less likely to streak, the taste won't be quite as good.

For triple-dipped berries, melt (separately) about 2 oz (60 g) bittersweet chocolate, 4 oz (125 g) milk chocolate and 6 oz (175 g) white chocolate. Dip the strawberries first into the white chocolate. Allow to set in the refrigerator. Then dip the berries halfway into the milk chocolate and allow to set. Finally, dip just the tip of the berries into the bittersweet chocolate, and allow to set.

12 oz	bittersweet or semisweet chocolate	375 g
16	large strawberries, cleaned	16

1. Melt chocolate gently over hot water or in the microwave. (When melting chocolate, always remove it from the heat before it is completely melted. Stir to complete the melting, so there is no chance of burning.)

2. Dip strawberries halfway in the chocolate and set on a waxed paper-lined baking sheet. Allow to set at room temperature, or in the refrigerator for 30 minutes.

5

Frozen Desserts

*I*CE cream may be my favorite food. I resisted making my own ice cream for years, because I was worried I wouldn't be able to stop eating it. But when I did finally start making my own, it actually helped me control my urge for ice cream, because I became far more discriminating.

Although there are ice cream mixtures that do not require an ice cream machine, most ice creams are easier to make, and have a better texture, if you have one.

Until recently you had to work relatively hard to make your own ice cream. Ice cream machines were either complicated to use, or very expensive. Homemade ice cream really became available to everyone when Donvier-style machines were introduced. They come in many different sizes and models, but they are based on a freezer-pack canister. You freeze the canister for eight hours or longer and then churn the ice cream in the frozen container. Although the ice cream is hand-cranked, you only have to crank it a few times every couple of minutes, and after twenty minutes your ice cream is ready.

These machines are reasonable in price, but they are not perfect. You cannot make batch after batch (the canister has to be refrozen in between, though you can buy extra canisters), and the ice cream sometimes crystallizes if you make it ahead and then transfer it to a container to store in the freezer. To avoid this problem I like to make the ice cream mixture itself ahead of time, without freezing it, and leave it in the refrigerator. Between the main course and dessert I bring the ice cream freezer to the table and let guests take turns cranking. (No one seems to mind participating!) Then I serve it right out of the container.

There are many different types of frozen desserts. Sorbets or ices are usually purees of fruit or concentrated juice with a sugar syrup and lemon juice. Granitas are similar to sorbets but are usually made from a juice or liquid with little or no syrup, and therefore they are slightly granular. Sherbets are made from a puree of fruit but with milk and/or egg whites added. Ice creams are made with cream and/or milk flavored with sugar, fruit or flavorings. Sometimes eggs or egg yolks are added. Ice cream can also be made with a custard base.

Frozen yogurt is yogurt frozen with sugar and fruit.

Parfaits, frozen soufflés, frozen mousses or semifreddos are made with whipped cream folded into a custard base and frozen without using an ice cream freezer.

Frozen Dessert Tips

• If you have an ice cream freezer, follow the directions that come with it. All ice cream machines vary slightly.

• No matter what frozen dessert you are making, make sure that the mixture is very cold before placing it in the machine to freeze. To cool the mixture quickly, place it in a large bowl set over a larger bowl of ice cubes and water. Stir to cool it even more quickly.

• If there is alcohol in the frozen dessert, it can slow down or impair the freezing. Only use small amounts of alcohol in frozen desserts and serve the rest poured over the finished dessert as a flavorful sauce.

• Add fruit or nuts to the ice cream toward the end of the freezing time. If added at the start, sometimes they sink to the bottom and can even prevent the paddle from churning properly.

• Although you may think whipping cream will make an ice cream richer and creamier, this isn't always the case. Because the ice cream is being churned, sometimes the mixture becomes too buttery and coarse in texture. I usually like to use a combination of milk and whipping cream instead.

• When making sorbets, a higher sugar syrup content usually results in a smoother finished product. If you only add fruit juice, coffee or a fruit puree, the results are still refreshing but more like the Italian granitas, which are more granular.

• If you do not have an ice cream freezer, there are many ways to make frozen desserts. The Italian semifreddos or the French frozen parfaits are based on custards with whipped cream folded in. The whipped cream keeps the mixture smooth and the results are very rich but great. Frozen desserts can also be made by placing the mixture in a cold metal pan. Partially freeze the mixture, then process in a food processor or beat with a mixer. Partially freeze again. Repeat this a few times before freezing completely. Another method is to freeze pieces of fresh fruit until solid and then puree in a food processor until creamy. Eat immediately.

• When I was growing up ice cream was always served in a bowl or cup, or maybe a wine glass. Now the style is to serve two or three oval scoops on a large dinner plate. Sprinkle fresh fruit on top, drizzle sauce over all and dust lightly with icing sugar. It is very easy, and really does look sensational.

• If you have a very cold freezer, remove the ice cream to the refrigerator 15 to 30 minutes before serving. Even though microwave books recommend the microwave for softening hard ice cream, you do have to be very careful not to overdo it.

• Ice cream can be shaped into scoops before a party, frozen on a baking sheet and assembled at the last minute.

• If you are storing ice cream, wrap it well. I find that homemade ice creams deteriorate rapidly after two or three weeks.

Caramel Ice Cream

*W*HEN *I first started the cooking school, I went to the south of France with Monda Rosenberg, food editor of* Chatelaine *magazine. In addition to taking cooking lessons with the famous cookbook author and teacher, Simone "Simca" Beck, we went to many restaurants. A caramel ice cream was one of the most delicious dishes I remember from that trip. It took me years of research (eating all the mistakes and close calls along the way, of course) to find that perfect balance of caramel and cream, but I think this is finally it! If you do not have an ice cream machine, just follow the directions at the end of the recipe. The texture will be slightly different, but it will still be very good.*

1 cup	granulated sugar	250 mL
3 tbsp	water	50 mL
1/2 cup	boiling water	125 mL
4	egg yolks	4
3/4 cup	light cream	175 mL
1 cup	whipping cream	250 mL
1 tsp	pure vanilla extract	5 mL

1. Place sugar and 3 tbsp (50 mL) water in a medium or large heavy saucepan. Cook, stirring, until liquid is clear and mixture just comes to the boil.

2. Have a cup of cold water and pastry brush at hand. Dip brush in water and brush down sides of pan where any sugar crystals remain. Do not worry if extra water runs into the sugar.

3. Cook mixture, without stirring, until a deep caramel color. Remove from heat.

4. Carefully, standing back and averting your face, pour in boiling water. Mixture may bubble up furiously; caramel may harden slightly. Stir to dissolve. Return to heat for a minute if necessary.

5. In bowl, beat egg yolks until light. Very slowly, whisk in hot caramel syrup. Beat until mixture is light and fluffy. Continue to beat until mixture is cool. (Placing the bowl over another bowl filled with ice cubes and water is a good way to cool it quickly.)

6. Stir in light cream, whipping cream and vanilla. Freeze in an ice cream machine according to manufacturer's directions. If you do not have an ice cream machine, do not add light and whipping creams and vanilla as instructed above. Instead, whip 1-3/4 cups (425 mL) whipping cream with vanilla until light and fold into cool egg-yolk mixture. Transfer to an ice cream mold or a stainless-steel bowl and freeze until firm.

A Lighter Side: If you have an ice cream machine, you can substitute milk for the light cream, and light cream for the whipping cream.

Raspberry Ice Cream

YIELD: Serves 6 to 8

*T*HIS *ice cream is very easy to make. Although it does not have a custard base, it does have a very soft, creamy texture. The raspberry seeds can be left in the mixture (some people say you then know for sure what you are eating!), but I like to strain them out. If you puree the berries in a blender or food processor, simply press the mixture through a sieve. Or use an old-fashioned food mill; it purees the berries and strains out the seeds at the same time.*

For an elegant but easy presentation, I serve the ice cream in three oval scoops radiating from the center of each plate. I spoon three marinated cherries with a little sauce between each scoop and place an edible flower in the center. Then I dust the outer rim of the plate with icing sugar. I use amarena cherries, available at some Italian ice cream shops, but any marinated fruit will work well.

4 cups	fresh raspberries, or 2 10 oz (300 g) packages frozen unsweetened raspberries	1 L
2	eggs	2
1-1/4 cups	granulated sugar	300 mL
1-1/2 cups	light cream	375 mL
1 cup	whipping cream	250 mL
1 tbsp	lemon juice	15 mL
1 tbsp	raspberry liqueur or raspberry jam	15 mL

1. Puree berries and strain out seeds.

2. In large bowl, beat eggs with sugar until very light — about 4 minutes with a hand beater or mixer. Beat in puree, light cream and whipping cream. Add lemon juice and liqueur.

3. Freeze in an ice cream machine according to manufacturer's directions. If you do not have an ice cream freezer, freeze in a flat metal pan until partially frozen, about 2 hours. Beat in food processor or with a mixer until smooth. Repeat this freezing and beating procedure two or three times before freezing completely.

A **Lighter Side**: Use milk or unflavored yogurt instead of the light cream and whipping cream.

Hazelnut Coffee Semifreddo with Brittle Chocolate Sauce

YIELD: Serves 8 to 10

I first discovered semifreddo (meaning "partially frozen") in Italy, and I fell in love with it. You don't even need an ice cream machine to make it. The sauce is the kind that hardens as it hits the ice cream.

6	egg yolks	6
2/3 cup	granulated sugar	150 mL
1/4 cup	extra-strong coffee or coffee liqueur	50 mL
1/4 cup	hazelnut liqueur or Amaretto	50 mL
2 cups	whipping cream	500 mL
1/2 cup	chopped toasted hazelnuts	125 mL
3 oz	bittersweet or semisweet chocolate, chopped	90 g
	Brittle Chocolate Sauce	
4 oz	bittersweet or semisweet chocolate	125 g
1/3 cup	whipping cream	75 mL
2 tbsp	unsalted butter	25 mL
1 tsp	pure vanilla extract	5 mL
	Garnish	
10	fresh strawberries	10
2 tbsp	sifted cocoa, approx.	25 mL

1. In bowl, combine egg yolks with sugar and beat until light and lemony. Whisk in coffee and hazelnut liqueur.

2. Set bowl over a saucepan of simmering water and cook, stirring constantly, until mixture has thickened. Remove from heat and cool. To cool it quickly, set bowl over a larger bowl of ice and water and whisk every 2 or 3 minutes.

3. In separate bowl, whip cream until light. Fold gently into cool custard base. Fold in nuts and chocolate.

4. Transfer mixture to an 8 × 4 inch (1.5 L) loaf pan that has been lined with plastic wrap. Wrap well and freeze for a few hours or overnight.

5. To make the sauce, combine chocolate with whipping cream in saucepan and cook gently until chocolate has melted and mixture is smooth. Stir in butter and vanilla. Add water to thin if necessary.

6. To serve, unmold semifreddo and slice. Place each slice on a dessert plate and drizzle with sauce on the diagonal. Place a strawberry on the side of each plate and dust sifted cocoa lightly over the plate.

Vanilla Bourbon Ice Cream with Pecan Caramel Sauce

*T*HIS *is a wonderful vanilla ice cream that can be made with or without the Bourbon. Any liqueur can be substituted, of course, and for a great vanilla flavor, try it plain. The texture of this ice cream is best if it is made in an ice cream machine.*

YIELD: Serves 8

2 cups	milk	500 mL
1	vanilla bean	1
6	egg yolks	6
1/2 cup	granulated sugar	125 mL
2 cups	whipping cream	500 mL
1/4 cup	Bourbon, rye or Scotch	50 mL
	Pecan Caramel Sauce (page 178)	

1. Place milk in saucepan. Split open vanilla bean and scrape seeds into milk. Heat gently until mixture comes to the boil. Simmer for 5 minutes. Strain milk. (Do not worry if tiny vanilla seeds remain.)

2. In bowl, beat egg yolks with sugar until pale and thick. Beat in hot vanilla/milk mixture. Return to saucepan and cook gently, stirring constantly, until mixture thickens slightly. Do not boil.

3. Stir in cream and Bourbon. Strain. Chill thoroughly.

4. When ice cream mixture is very cold, place in an ice cream machine and freeze according to manufacturer's directions.

5. Serve with Pecan Caramel Sauce.

A **Lighter Side:** Use milk or light cream instead of whipping cream. Use half the liqueur.

Grand Marnier Ice Cream Cake

YIELD: Serves 10 to 12

*A*LTHOUGH *this spectacular dessert takes time to make, it can all be prepared ahead of time. The ice cream can also be served on its own.*

The further ahead you make this, the better you should wrap it. It keeps well, but it could easily acquire a "freezer" taste.

Although Grand Marnier is expensive, it does have a wonderful flavor that will make this dessert extra special. Serve wedges with some Berry Berry Sauce (see page 172) on one side and a whole strawberry on the other. Dust the cake, fruit and rim of the plate with sifted icing sugar.

	Meringue	
4	egg whites	4
1/2 cup	fruit sugar	125 mL
1/2 cup	sifted icing sugar	125 mL
1/2 cup	ground toasted almonds	125 mL
1 tbsp	cornstarch	15 mL
	Grand Marnier Ice Cream	
1 cup	granulated sugar	250 mL
1/4 cup	water	50 mL
6	egg yolks	6
1/2 cup	sifted icing sugar, divided	125 mL
1/2 cup	Grand Marnier	125 mL
3 cups	whipping cream	750 mL
2 tsp	pure vanilla extract	10 mL

1. Preheat oven to 275° F (140° C). Line two baking sheets with parchment paper. (Butter the baking sheets very lightly just to hold the paper in place.) Trace a 10 inch (25 cm) circle on each sheet.

2. To make the meringue, beat egg whites until light. Slowly beat in fruit sugar. Continue to beat until stiff.

3. In separate bowl, combine icing sugar with nuts and cornstarch. Mix well. Fold into egg-white mixture.

4. Transfer meringue to a piping tube and pipe meringue within the traced circles. (If you do not have a piping tube, spread meringue as evenly as possible with a spatula.)

5. Bake for 2 to 3 hours, or until meringues are dry and very lightly browned. Turn off oven and let cool in oven.

6. To make ice cream, stir granulated sugar and water together in a heavy saucepan. Cook, stirring, until sugar dissolves. Without stirring, cook until mixture reaches 240° F (115° C) — soft ball stage.

7. In large bowl, with an electric mixer, beat egg yolks with 1/4 cup (50 mL) icing sugar until light. Slowly beat in syrup. Continue to beat until mixture is cool and very light. Stir in 1/4 cup (50 mL) Grand Marnier.

8. In separate bowl, whip cream until light. Beat in vanilla and remaining Grand Marnier. Fold cream into yolk base.

9. Trim meringues to fit a 10 inch (25 cm) springform pan (the meringues may have spread when baked). Place one meringue in bottom of pan. Spoon ice cream mixture over and top with second meringue. (If there is too much ice cream, freeze excess separately for a "chef's treat.") Freeze. When frozen, wrap well.

10. To serve, unwrap and unmold. (Use either side up, whichever is nicest.) Dust top with remaining icing sugar.

A Lighter Side: Instead of the Grand Marnier ice cream, use a sorbet (or ice cream made with milk).

Raspberry Sorbet

*T*HIS *is great on its own for a light dessert, or with just about anything deep, dark and chocolaty.*

YIELD: Serves 6 to 8

3/4 cup	granulated sugar	175 mL
3/4 cup	water	175 mL
2	10 oz (300 g) packages frozen raspberries, individually quick frozen, or 4 cups (1 L) fresh	2
2 tbsp	lemon juice	25 mL

1. Bring sugar and water to a boil in a heavy saucepan. Cook for 1 minute. Cool.

2. Defrost berries and puree. Strain out the seeds. (A food mill will puree and strain all at once.)

3. Combine raspberry puree with syrup and lemon juice.

4. Freeze in an ice cream machine according to manufacturer's directions. If you do not have an ice cream machine, place mixture in a shallow metal pan. Partially freeze, about 2 hours, then beat with a mixer or in a food processor. Repeat this two or three times and then freeze completely.

Zabaione Semifreddo

YIELD: Serves 8
to 10

*Z*ABAIONE *is so soothing and creamy that I always feel better after I have eaten some — even if I felt fine to begin with! This frozen version is perfect for entertaining, as it can easily be made ahead of time. The version below is plain, but you could fold in 1/2 cup (125 mL) chopped bittersweet chocolate, and/or chopped toasted almonds and/or diced pound cake. As with most semifreddos (see page 129), you do not need an ice cream machine to make this.*

5	egg yolks	5
1/2 cup	granulated sugar	125 mL
3/4 cup	dry Marsala	175 mL
1/4 cup	Cognac or brandy	50 mL
1-1/2 cups	whipping cream	375 mL
	Fresh strawberries	

1. In bowl, beat egg yolks with sugar until light and lemony. Stir in Marsala and Cognac. Place bowl over pot of gently simmering water and cook, stirring constantly, until mixture thickens. Do not let mixture come to a boil, or eggs may curdle.

2. Cool mixture completely. If you are in a hurry, set bowl over a larger bowl filled with ice and water. Stir occasionally. Mixture will cool much more quickly this way.

3. Whip cream until thick. Fold gently into cool custard base. (At this point, fold in any chocolate, nuts or cake if you are using them.) Spoon mixture into a 9 × 5 inch (2 L) loaf pan, bowl or mold lined with plastic wrap.

4. Freeze for 4 to 5 hours or until firm. If you are making this more than one day ahead of time, be sure to wrap it tightly.

5. Serve in slices with whole strawberries as a garnish.

Espresso Ice Cream

*T*HIS *ice cream has a custard base, so the texture is best when it is made in an ice cream machine. Be sure the custard is completely chilled before pouring it into the machine, otherwise it will not freeze as well. I often stir in 1 cup (250 mL) chopped bittersweet or semisweet chocolate just before the ice cream is finished. For a wonderful sundae, serve with caramel sauce (see page 178) and bananas.*

YIELD: Serves 6 to 8

2 cups	milk	500 mL
3 tbsp	espresso coffee beans, coarsely ground	50 mL
6	egg yolks	6
1/2 cup	granulated sugar	125 mL
1 tbsp	instant coffee powder, preferably espresso	15 mL
1 cup	whipping cream	250 mL

1. In saucepan, bring milk and ground coffee beans to the boil. Remove from heat and allow to rest for 5 minutes. Strain through a fine strainer, cheesecloth or paper towel-lined strainer. Do not worry if little flecks of coffee remain in the mixture.

2. In bowl, beat egg yolks with sugar until light and lemony. Beat in coffee-flavored milk. Return to saucepan and add instant coffee. Cook over medium-low heat until mixture is slightly thickened, but do not boil.

3. Stir in whipping cream and chill.

4. Freeze in an ice cream machine according to manufacturer's directions.

A **Lighter Side:** Use milk or light cream instead of whipping cream. Use four egg yolks instead of six.

Chocolate Truffle Raspberry Ice Cream

YIELD: Serves 8 to 10

*O**F** course you can make this double dessert with flavors other than raspberry, but I think the raspberry flavor is sensational. The creamy bits of truffle throughout the ice cream are so seductive, it is hard to stop eating it. Serve as is in wine glasses or on a bed of raspberry sauce (see page 179) with some fresh raspberries dotted through the sauce.*

3 cups	milk	750 mL
4	egg yolks	4
1/2 cup	granulated sugar	125 mL
6 oz	bittersweet or semisweet chocolate	175 g
1 cup	whipping cream	250 mL
1/4 cup	raspberry liqueur	50 mL
1 tsp	pure vanilla extract	5 mL
	Truffles	
6 oz	bittersweet or semisweet chocolate, chopped	175 g
1/4 cup	unsalted butter	50 mL
1	egg yolk	1
2 tbsp	raspberry liqueur	25 mL
	Sifted cocoa	

1. Heat milk in saucepan.

2. In bowl, beat egg yolks with granulated sugar until light. Slowly beat in hot milk, Return mixture to saucepan and cook gently until barely thickened, about 5 minutes on medium-low.

3. Chop chocolate and place in large bowl. Pour hot cream mixture over chocolate. Allow to rest for 2 minutes. Whisk to melt chocolate. Stir in cream, liqueur and vanilla. Chill mixture thoroughly.

4. To make truffle mixture, melt chocolate with butter in double boiler over simmering water. Whisk in egg yolk and liqueur. Chill.

5. Shape half of mixture into tiny 1/2 inch (1 cm) trufflets and remaining mixture into larger 1 inch (2.5 cm) truffles. Freeze tiny ones. Roll larger ones in cocoa and refrigerate.

6. Freeze ice cream mixture in ice cream machine according to manufacturer's directions. When almost frozen, add trufflets and stir in. Serve ice cream with one large truffle on each serving.

A Lighter Side: Use milk instead of cream, and use two egg yolks instead of four.

6

Fruit Desserts

NOTHING gives your table a more seasonal flavor than fresh fruits and vegetables. For many people, a rhubarb dessert means that spring has arrived; and what could be more summery than a berry pie or shortcake. In the autumn, pears and plums signal cooler days, and our trusty Canadian apple is on hand all winter.

Although in many cities you can now find imported fresh strawberries (and sometimes even raspberries and peaches) in December and January, they are terribly expensive, and sometimes terrible-tasting, too. But more than that, it just doesn't seem right. Somehow I feel more in touch with nature when my table is in season.

So always choose the freshest fruit possible, and remember that the quality of the ingredients you use will be reflected in the finished product.

Fruit Tips

• My favorite cooking apple is Spy. Many books recommend Granny Smith apples, but I find them too tart and watery for baking. In different areas of the country, other good cooking apples are available. Golden Delicious are usually easy to find everywhere, and they work well in cooking, although they are not my favorite apples for eating.

● My favorite blueberries are the tiny ones I buy on the roadside coming home from cottage country in August. They are harder to clean and sort than the larger, more watery blueberries, but they have such an intense flavor that they are worth the trouble.

● Jacques Marie is one of my favorite chefs. He was my chef instructor at George Brown College in Toronto, twenty years ago (when we were both very, very young), and he now teaches wine seminars at my cooking school. He once told me that the way to tell a good cantaloupe is to first find the female ones — the cantaloupes with the large stem ends. Then sniff the end. If it has a strong cantaloupe smell, the fruit is ripe. I still don't know whether Jacques was pulling my leg when he told me this, but I do know that I always get a good cantaloupe if I follow his advice.

● To make melon balls, cut a melon in half. Position the melon baller on the flat cut surface and press it down with your thumb so that the handle of the instrument is perpendicular to the melon. Turn it around and lift it out. You should have a perfect melon ball. (Unfortunately, you probably won't get a lot of absolutely perfect balls out of one melon.)

● There is nothing like the flavor and texture of fresh raspberries (although they are usually awfully expensive). Most of the time I do not even wash raspberries, because they are so delicate. Frozen raspberries can be used in a sauce, but they do not work well as a garnish or in fruit salads. When I want to make a raspberry sauce, I try to use the individually quick frozen raspberries, since they do not contain extra sugar or liquid. If I can only find raspberries frozen in syrup, I defrost them and strain them, reserving the juice. I puree the berries through a food mill (which purees and strains at the same time) and then add back juice to reach the consistency I want. If you do not have a food mill, puree the berries in a blender or food processor and then press the mixture through a strainer. (If you are using fresh raspberries, you can thin the sauce with orange juice if necessary.)

● Always hull strawberries after cleaning. I prefer to pat the berries clean with damp paper towels, but if you must wash them, rinse quickly so they do not become water-logged. Pat dry with paper towels and then hull. When dipping strawberries into chocolate, do not rinse unless necessary, and dry them well before dipping!

● I do not usually freeze desserts that contain fresh fruit. Because of the moisture in the fruit, ice crystals form, and when the dessert is defrosted, it becomes watery. If I am stirring fresh fruit into ice cream, I usually cut it into tiny bits to prevent it from becoming too icy.

• If I want to prevent fruit from discoloring, I sometimes toss the cut fruit with a little lemon juice. If the fruit is baked (such as a cobbler or crisp), it doesn't usually matter if the fruit discolors a little. In fruit salads, the "dressing" will often help prevent discoloration. As a further precaution, add any fruit that may discolor shortly before serving. If some fruits, such as strawberries, are left in a marinade overnight, they usually become discolored and soggy. These fruits should be added to a salad only a few hours before serving.

Antipasta Fruit Plate

T HIS is a wonderful idea for a light dessert. Serve each guest a plate of mixed fruit slices, cheese and a homemade cookie. Style it well and it will look like a million, be low in calories and really easy to put together. You can use any combination of fruits and cheese — I have just given a few ideas.

YIELD: Serves 8

1	large bunch fresh mint	1
16	fresh strawberries	16
1	ripe mango, peeled and sliced	1
1	small honeydew melon, peeled and sliced	1
8 oz	seedless red grapes, separated into 8 small bunches	250 g
8 oz	Brie, Camembert or Cambazola	250 g
8	Hazelnut Biscotti (page 114)	8

1. Arrange mint on one half of each plate. Arrange 2 strawberries, a few slices of mango and honeydew and a bunch of grapes on top of the mint.

2. Slice the cheese into 16 thin pieces. Arrange 2 slices on each plate beside the fruit. Place a cookie beside the cheese.

Strawberry Shortcakes with Lemon Cream

YIELD: Serves 6 to 8

A picture is worth a thousand words, which is why we chose this dessert for our cover shot. We felt it represented the essence of what this cookbook is all about.

I didn't think anything could beat old-fashioned strawberry shortcake made with whipped cream. But after you taste these shortcakes, I think you'll agree there's something to be said for trying new things, like this fabulous lemon cream. The idea for the lemon cream itself came from Maureen Lollar, who has been working with me at the cooking school for eight years. We also use it as a filling for crêpes and tart shells.

	Biscuits	
2 cups	all-purpose flour	500 mL
3 tbsp	granulated sugar, divided	50 mL
1 tbsp	baking powder	15 mL
1 tsp	finely grated lemon peel	5 mL
1/2 tsp	baking soda	2 mL
pinch	salt	pinch
1/2 cup	unsalted butter, cold	125 mL
1-1/2 cups	sour cream	375 mL
2 tbsp	milk, approx.	25 mL
	Filling	
4 cups	fresh strawberries, hulled and halved	1 L
1/2 cup	lemon juice, divided	125 mL
3/4 cup	granulated sugar, divided	175 mL
3	egg yolks	3
1/3 cup	unsalted butter, melted	75 mL
1 tsp	finely grated lemon peel	5 mL
1-1/2 cups	whipping cream	375 mL
	Sifted icing sugar	

1. Preheat oven to 425° F (220° C). Line a baking sheet with parchment paper.

2. To prepare biscuits, combine flour, 2 tbsp (25 mL) granulated sugar, baking powder, lemon peel, baking soda and salt in large bowl. Cut in butter until it is in tiny bits. (This can be done in a food processor fitted with the steel knife.) Add sour cream and work in gently to form a dough.

3. Pat or roll dough about 1 to 1-1/2 inches (2.5 to 4 cm) thick on a floured board. Cut into six to eight 4 inch (10 cm) squares. Place on baking sheet. Brush with milk and sprinkle with remaining 1 tbsp (15 mL) granulated sugar.

4. Bake for 15 minutes, or until puffed and golden. Cool on wire racks.

5. For filling, combine berries with 3 tbsp (50 mL) lemon juice and 1/4 cup (50 mL) granulated sugar. Let sit for 30 minutes.

6. Beat egg yolks with remaining 1/2 cup (125 mL) granulated sugar in medium saucepan. Whisk in remaining 1/3 cup (75 mL) lemon juice, butter and peel. Stirring constantly, cook until thickened but do not boil. Transfer to a large bowl and cool to room temperature.

7. In separate bowl, whip cream until thick. Fold gently into cool lemon mixture.

8. To assemble, halve biscuits horizontally. Place bottoms on dessert plates. Top with sliced berries, allowing juices to soak into cake and run onto plate. Spoon on cream mixture and place biscuit tops, slightly lopsided, over cream. Dust tops lightly with sifted icing sugar.

A **Lighter Side**: Instead of lemon cream filling, use light sour cream or unflavored yogurt, sweetened to taste.

Sweet and Sour Strawberries

*T*HE *mysterious flavor of the vinegar is a surprise to anyone who tastes these wonderful tart berries. My favorite vinegars for this are balsamic or raspberry, but lemon juice is also great. I only like to marinate the berries for four or five hours before serving, as they tend to lose their color and texture if left to stand longer. Leftovers, however, are still very edible the next day.*

Serve these berries over ice cream or a fruit sorbet, inside a cantaloupe half, or puree and freeze in an ice cream machine for a tangy granita — a crystally frozen dessert. Or you can serve them with shortcake and crème fraiche for a nouvelle strawberry shortcake.

YIELD: Serves 4 to 6

4 cups	fresh strawberries	1 L
3 tbsp	raspberry vinegar	50 mL
3 tbsp	granulated sugar	50 mL

1. Wash and hull berries. Quarter them if they are large, or halve them if they are small.

2. Sprinkle with vinegar and sugar. Combine well. Allow to marinate for at least 30 minutes, or up to 4 hours.

Rhubarb Cobbler

YIELD: Serves 8
to 10

*T*HIS *is an old favorite that is always in fashion. Do not worry if the fruit mixture is a bit runny when you take it out of the oven; it will firm up a tiny bit when it cools. I prefer the rhubarb juices runny, but if you like, you can add 2 tbsp (25 mL) all-purpose flour to the rhubarb mixture at the start.*

Serve this with a scoop of vanilla ice cream, dusted with icing sugar. Garnish with an edible flower or strawberry. If you use other fruit, such as berries, omit the brown sugar.

2 lb	rhubarb, cut into 1 inch (2.5 cm) pieces	1 kg
3/4 cup	granulated sugar	175 mL
1/2 cup	brown sugar	125 mL
2 tbsp	unsalted butter, cut into bits	25 mL
	Topping	
2 cups	all-purpose flour	500 mL
pinch	salt	pinch
1 tbsp	baking powder	15 mL
1/4 cup	granulated sugar	50 mL
2 tsp	finely grated orange peel	10 mL
1 tsp	ground cinnamon	5 mL
1/2 cup	unsalted butter, cut into pieces	125 mL
1 cup	milk	250 mL

1. Preheat oven to 400° F (200° C). Butter a 12 × 8 inch (3 L) baking dish.

2. In bowl, combine rhubarb with sugars and butter. Spread over bottom of pan.

3. For topping, in large bowl, combine flour with salt, baking powder, sugar, orange peel and cinnamon. Cut in butter until it is in tiny bits. Sprinkle mixture with milk. Stir together just until a heavy batter is formed.

4. Drop batter by spoonfuls over top of rhubarb and spread to cover surface.

5. Bake for 35 to 40 minutes, or until biscuit is browned and fruit is tender. Allow to cool before serving.

Apple Oatmeal Cobbler

*T*HE *intriguing taste of the cardamom and the oatmeal in the batter make this cobbler a little different. It tastes wonderful as is, but I love it with a little vanilla or cinnamon ice cream!*

YIELD: Serves 6 to 8

5	apples	5
1/3 cup	brown sugar	75 mL
2 tsp	ground cinnamon	10 mL
1/2 tsp	ground cardamom	2 mL
pinch	ground nutmeg	pinch
2 tbsp	unsalted butter, cold, cut into bits	25 mL
	Topping	
1-1/2 cups	all-purpose flour	375 mL
1/2 cup	rolled oats	125 mL
1/3 cup	granulated sugar, divided	75 mL
1 tbsp	baking powder	15 mL
pinch	salt	pinch
1/2 cup	unsalted butter, cold	125 mL
3/4 cup	milk	175 mL
2 tbsp	cream	25 mL
1/4 cup	sliced almonds	50 mL

1. Preheat oven to 375° F (190° C). Butter an 8 or 9 inch (2 or 2.5 L) baking dish.

2. Peel apples. Halve, core and slice thinly.

3. Toss apples, brown sugar, cinnamon, cardamom, nutmeg and butter. Place in the bottom of baking dish.

4. Prepare topping by combining flour, rolled oats, 1/4 cup (50 mL) granulated sugar, baking powder and salt. Cut in butter until it is in tiny bits. Sprinkle milk over flour mixture and gather together with a wooden spoon. Dough will be sticky.

5. Spoon dough over apples and spread to cover the surface as much as possible.

6. Brush topping with cream and sprinkle with remaining 2 tbsp (25 mL) granulated sugar. Sprinkle with almonds.

7. Bake for 40 to 45 minutes, or until top is lightly browned and apples are tender. Allow to rest for at least 15 minutes before serving.

Pear Custard Crisp

YIELD: Serves 6
to 8

*T*HIS *is a very unusual crisp. The fruit is covered with a custard sauce, sprinkled with gingersnap crumbs and then baked. It's a new old-fashioned dessert.*

2	eggs	2
1/2 cup	granulated sugar	125 mL
1/4 cup	all-purpose flour	50 mL
2 cups	milk, hot	500 mL
1/2 cup	whipping cream	125 mL
1 tsp	pure vanilla extract	5 mL
1/4 cup	unsalted butter, melted	50 mL
1-1/2 cups	gingersnap cookie crumbs, approx. 6 oz (175 g)	375 mL
6	ripe pears, preferably Bartlett	6
2 tbsp	brown sugar	25 mL
1/2 tsp	ground cinnamon	2 mL

1. Preheat oven to 350° F (180° C).

2. To prepare custard, beat eggs with granulated sugar in a heavy saucepan. Beat in flour. Slowly whisk in hot milk. Stirring constantly, cook over medium heat until sauce thickens and just comes to a boil. Stir in cream and bring to a boil again. Remove from heat. Stir in vanilla.

3. Using some of the melted butter, butter an 8 cup (2 L) baking dish or individual baking dishes and sprinkle with some of the gingersnap crumbs.

4. Peel, halve, core and slice pears. In a bowl, combine pears with brown sugar and cinnamon. Spoon into baking dish. Pour custard over the pears.

5. Combine remaining butter with remaining crumbs and sprinkle over custard. Place pan on a baking sheet.

6. Bake for 35 to 40 minutes, or until top is crisp, pears are tender and custard is bubbling. Cool for at least 10 minutes before serving.

Dried Fruit Crisp

*I*N the summer there are so many fruit desserts to choose from, but choices in the winter are more limited. Here is a traditional apple crisp with a twist of added pears and dried fruits. Serve as is or with a little caramel or vanilla ice cream (pages 130 and 133).

YIELD: Serves 8 to 10

4	large apples, preferably Spy or Golden Delicious	4
2	pears, preferably Bartlett or Bosc	2
1/2 cup	dried apricots, halved	125 mL
1/2 cup	prunes or dates, halved	125 mL
1/2 cup	raisins or currants	125 mL
2 tbsp	unsalted butter, cut into bits	25 mL
2 tbsp	brown sugar	25 mL
2 tbsp	lemon juice	25 mL
	Topping	
3/4 cup	all-purpose or whole wheat flour	175 mL
1/2 cup	rolled oats	125 mL
1/2 cup	chopped walnuts or pecans	125 mL
1/2 cup	granulated sugar	125 mL
1/4 cup	brown sugar	50 mL
1 tbsp	ground cinnamon	15 mL
1/2 cup	unsalted butter, cold	125 mL

1. Preheat oven to 375° F (190° C). Butter a 13 × 9 inch (3.5 L) baking dish.

2. Peel, halve, core and slice the apples and pears. Place in a large bowl. Add the apricots, prunes and raisins. Toss together.

3. Sprinkle fruit with butter bits, brown sugar and lemon juice. Toss well. Arrange in bottom of prepared dish.

4. To make topping, combine flour with rolled oats, nuts, sugars and cinnamon. Stir together well. Cut in butter until it is in tiny bits. Sprinkle mixture evenly over fruit.

5. Bake for 50 to 60 minutes, or until apples are very tender. Serve warm or cold.

Gingered Fruit Salad

YIELD: Serves 6 to 8

*F*RESH *ginger adds a zing to a traditional fruit salad. This is really easy to make but has a very sophisticated and exotic flavor. If you like, you can add mango and passionfruit as well as the fruits suggested.*

2	oranges	2
1-1/2 cups	seedless green grapes	375 mL
2 cups	fresh strawberries, hulled and halved	500 mL
2	bananas	2
2 tbsp	orange marmalade	25 mL
1 tbsp	honey	15 mL
1/3 cup	orange juice	75 mL
1 tsp	grated fresh ginger	5 mL

1. To section the oranges easily, cut a slice off top and bottom and stand on a cutting board. Starting at the top end, cut off peel, exposing the orange segments. Continue until orange is completely peeled. Then, holding orange in your hand, cut out segments from between the membranes. Work over large bowl to catch any juice. Add grapes and strawberries. Peel and slice bananas. Combine well with other fruit.

2. Whisk marmalade with honey and juice. Stir in ginger.

3. Combine dressing with fruit. Allow to marinate for at least 30 minutes or up to 4 hours. Serve cold or at room temperature.

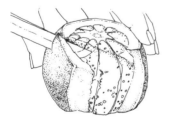
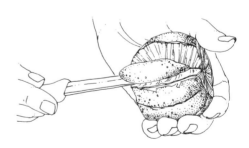

Melon and Blueberry Salad with Lime

A LTHOUGH *the combination of green and bluish-purple may sound odd, this salad is gorgeous to look at and even nicer to eat. If you cannot find any ripe honeydew melons, use cantaloupe melons instead. Strawberries are also a colorful and delicious addition.*

YIELD: Serves 6 to 8

1	large honeydew melon	1
2 cups	blueberries	500 mL
1/4 cup	lime juice	50 mL
1 tsp	finely grated lime peel	5 mL
2 tbsp	dark rum	25 mL
2 tbsp	apricot jam or jelly	25 mL

1. Cut melon in half and discard seeds. Cut melon into cubes or into balls using a melon baller, and place in large bowl.

2. Wash and sort through blueberries. Combine with melon.

3. Whisk lime juice together with peel, rum and jam.

4. Toss with fruit. Allow to marinate for at least 30 minutes or up to overnight. Serve cold or at room temperature.

Winter Fruit Compote

YIELD: Serves 8

IN the winter, when you do not have a large variety of fresh fruit, try this lovely compote of dried fruits. It can be served as is, but it also makes a fabulous ice cream topping. I even serve it instead of maple syrup over pancakes or waffles. Slices of fresh pears and apples can be added to this as well.

1 cup	orange juice	250 mL
1/2 cup	ruby port	125 mL
1/4 cup	honey	50 mL
1	cinnamon stick, broken	1
6	whole cloves	6
3	slices lemon, peels removed	3
2 cups	dried prunes	500 mL
2 cups	dried apricots	500 mL
1 cup	dried figs	250 mL
	Water	

1. Place orange juice, port, honey, cinnamon stick, cloves and lemon slices in a large saucepan and bring to a boil.

2. Add dried fruit and just enough water to cover.

3. Bring to a boil and then simmer gently for 7 to 10 minutes, or until fruit is tender but does not fall apart. Serve warm or cold.

Orange Baked Pears

YIELD: Serves 6

THIS is a warm, cozy, "lite" dessert. You could also slice the pears and serve them with a pear or lemon sorbet for something more sophisticated but not too rich.

6	pears, preferably Bartlett	6
1/2 cup	orange juice	125 mL
3 tbsp	orange liqueur	50 mL
2 tbsp	honey	25 mL
1 tsp	finely grated orange peel	5 mL
1/4 tsp	ground cinnamon	1 mL
1/4 tsp	ground cardamom, optional	1 mL

1. Preheat oven to 350° F (180° C).

2. Peel pears. Cut in half. Remove cores (a melon baller does this very attractively). Arrange pears in a single layer (or slightly overlapping) in 13 × 9 inch (3.5 L) baking dish, cut side up.

3. Combine orange juice with liqueur, honey, peel, cinnamon and cardamom. Pour over pears.

4. Cover pears tightly and baked for 30 to 45 minutes, or until pears are tender when pierced with a fork. Serve warm.

Piña Colada Fruit Cocktail

C OCKTAIL drinks have become very popular again. Fuzzy Navels, French Kisses (and much more daring!) have taken over the bar scene. And piña coladas in every flavor imaginable are some of the best sellers.

For a change, serve a dessert cocktail. It won't ruin your guests' appetites, and it will send everyone home in a rather good mood. Look for canned cream of coconut in the beverage section of the supermarket or in the specialty department (the unused cream of coconut can be frozen for future use).

YIELD: Serves 6 to 8

1	pineapple	1
1	ripe mango	1
1	ripe papaya	1
2	kiwi fruit	2
2 cups	fresh strawberries	500 mL
1/2 cup	pineapple juice	125 mL
1/3 cup	canned cream of coconut	75 mL
1/3 cup	dark rum	75 mL
1/2 cup	grated unsweetened coconut, toasted	125 mL

1. Peel and dice pineapple, mango and papaya. Peel kiwi fruit and cut into large pieces. Hull strawberries and cut in half. Combine all fruit in a large bowl and toss gently together.

2. Blend pineapple juice with cream of coconut and rum. Pour over fruit and allow to marinate for 30 minutes or up to 4 hours.

3. Serve fruit cocktail in cocktail glasses with toasted coconut sprinkled on top.

Mixed Daiquiri Fruit Cocktail

YIELD: Serves 6 to 8

*T*HIS *is what you call a real fruit cocktail! If any the fruits listed below are not available, just use fruits you like that are easy to find. The orange and lime juices should prevent the bananas from darkening.*

Fruit sugar is used in the dressing, since it blends into cold liquids more easily than granulated sugar. You can buy it prepared, or make it by whizzing regular sugar in the blender or food processor for 20 to 30 seconds.

If you are making this more than an hour ahead of time, add the bananas and strawberries just before serving.

2 cups	fresh strawberries	500 mL
3	peaches	3
3	oranges	3
2	bananas	2
1 cup	blueberries	250 mL
1 cup	raspberries	250 mL
1/3 cup	lime juice	75 mL
1/3 cup	fruit sugar	75 mL
1/3 cup	dark rum	75 mL
3 tbsp	orange liqueur	50 mL

1. Hull strawberries. Cut into halves or quarters, depending on their size.

2. Peel peaches by dipping them into boiling water for 30 seconds, cooling and slipping off skins. Cut into large chunks (similar in size to strawberries). Combine with strawberries in a large bowl.

3. Peel and section oranges over bowl of fruit to catch any juices (see page 148). Peel and slice bananas. Combine with fruit. Stir blueberries and raspberries very gently into fruit mixture.

4. Combine lime juice and sugar until sugar dissolves. Add rum and liqueur.

5. Stir dressing into fruit and allow to marinate for 30 minutes. Serve in cocktail glasses.

7

Desserts

WHEN I was in school, I always got confused about the spelling of words like dessert and desert, dinner and diner, filet and fillet. The dessert/desert problem was solved for me when a friend pointed out that you'd always want two desserts, but you would only want to cross the desert once! I haven't had a problem since.

The recipes in this chapter cover a wide range, and some of my favorites are here. They include classic custards like rich Coffee Crème Brûlée (page 167) or Crème Caramel (page 166), fashionable desserts like Tiramisu (page 171), and a few of my favorite soufflé and crêpe recipes. Soufflés and crêpes seem to intimidate many cooks, but they are actually very easy, especially if you follow a few basic techniques.

• Cold soufflés are actually mousses and not traditional soufflés. They are usually based on a rich gelatin, fruit or cream mixture and are never actually baked. To make a mousse look like a soufflé, make a collar around a small soufflé dish. To make a collar, double over a large piece of heavy-duty foil. Wrap it around the soufflé dish, tucking the ends under the bottom of the dish as shown. After the mixture has been refrigerated or frozen for a few hours, carefully remove the collar.

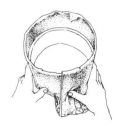

• If you are making a hot soufflé, allow the base to cool to lukewarm before folding in the egg whites. If you have made the base ahead of time and it is cold, warm it gently before folding in the egg whites.

• When beating egg whites, do not overbeat them. They should be light and fluffy. If you add sugar to egg whites, add it gradually after they are opaque. When egg whites are beaten correctly, you should be able to turn the bowl upside down without the whites falling out.

• When folding beaten egg whites into a heavier mixture, always stir about one-quarter of the egg whites into the base first, to lighten it. Then lightly fold in the remaining whites. It doesn't matter whether you put the remaining whites on the base or the lightened base on the whites — I usually use the bigger bowl.

• When folding, run your spatula down through the middle of the mixture and bring it toward you along the bottom and side of the bowl. With your opposite hand, turn the bowl while you are folding, so the mixture is folded in on all sides. If you want your soufflé to rise straight and tall, do not overfold; even if there are a few streaks of egg white still remaining, stop folding after about twelve folds. (If you are making a jelly-roll type of soufflé, then fold the mixtures together lightly but completely.)

• If you want a soufflé to puff spectacularly, add a few extra egg whites. (If you have six egg yolks in the soufflé, you could add up to nine egg whites.)

• Once the soufflé is in its dish, you can actually leave it for an hour or two before baking it. It may not rise quite as high as if you baked it right away, but it will still work well.

• Once baked, a soufflé should be served immediately (the rule is that guests wait for a soufflé because a soufflé will never wait for the guests). Bring the soufflé to the table immediately. Be organized. The faster you serve it, the better.

• If you want a soufflé to be dry in the center, bake it 5 minutes longer than a recipe suggests. Many chefs like soufflés that are creamy in the center; this acts as a sauce for the firmer outside edges. Serve some of the sauce part with some of the firmer portion. If you bake the soufflé until it is dry, you can serve a fruit puree, ice cream sauce or custard sauce with it if you wish.

• A crêpe batter is usually a thin, unleavened pancake batter. You can make crêpes a day ahead and refrigerate or freeze them for a few months. I find that when crêpes are frozen, they get a bit rubbery in texture, so I use frozen ones only if they are going to be "cooked" again or sauced.

• You can buy special crêpe pans, but an omelet pan works well. I usually use an 8 inch (20 cm) pan. Unless the pan is nonstick, it should be seasoned first. To season a pan, half-fill it with vegetable oil and heat gently for about 15 minutes. Let oil cool, then reheat. Repeat this four or five times. (Brush sides of pan with oil occasionally). Pour oil out of pan (if it is clean, it can be reused). After the initial seasoning, do not wash the pan, but use oil and/or salt (salt acts as an abrasive) to clean it. Do not use the pan for anything besides omelets and/or crêpes. If your pan begins to stick again after a while, just reseason it.

• Use unsalted or clarified butter to cook crêpes; they will be less likely to stick. I usually heat the pan, add a little butter, heat it, and then add about 1/4 cup (50 mL) batter. I cook one side and then the other of this test crêpe. If the crêpe sticks, I eat it, and then rub the trouble spot on the pan with some salt before trying again.

• Once the pan is working properly, spoon about 1/2 cup (125 mL) batter into the pan. Swirl it around to cover the bottom and a little way up the sides, then pour any extra batter back into the batter bowl. Cook the first side until it browns, then run a knife around the edge and flip the crêpe. Cook the second side just a little — it will never be as pretty as the first.

• Put the filling on the second side of the crêpes so that the nice side shows.

• Stack crêpes as they are cooked. If you are freezing them, place a piece of waxed paper between each one so they can be removed from the freezer as you need them.

Charlotte Basket with White Chocolate Mousse

YIELD: Serves 8 to 10

*W*HENEVER *I see this dessert I just think it is so pretty and romantic looking. It is perfect for dessert, of course, but also charming for a wedding shower or special party. Fresh flowers look flirtatious around the outside, mingled with the strawberries (make sure the flowers are edible ones).*

	White Chocolate Mousse	
12 oz	white chocolate	375 g
4 oz	cream cheese	125 g
1/4 cup	granulated sugar	50 mL
1 tsp	pure vanilla extract	5 mL
1/4 cup	orange liqueur	50 mL
2 cups	whipping cream	500 mL
6 oz	ladyfingers, commercial or homemade (page 110), about 24	175 g
2 tbsp	orange liqueur	25 mL
2 cups	fresh strawberries	500 mL
6 oz	white chocolate	175 g
	Sifted icing sugar	

1. To make white chocolate mousse, chop white chocolate coarsely. Very carefully, melt in the top of a double boiler over gently simmering water. Allow chocolate to cool slightly.

2. Meanwhile, in large bowl, beat cheese until light. Beat in granulated sugar. Add vanilla and 1/4 cup (50 mL) liqueur. Slowly beat in melted white chocolate.

3. In separate bowl, whip cream until light. Stir about one-third of whipped cream into white chocolate base to lighten the texture and then fold in remaining cream.

4. Line an 8 cup (2 L) soufflé dish or an 8 inch (20 cm) springform pan with plastic wrap. Brush flat side of ladyfingers with 2 tbsp (25 mL) orange liqueur. Arrange ladyfingers up sides of pan with rounded sides next to pan. Cut ladyfingers into spokes to line bottom.

5. Gently spoon mousse mixture into lined pan. Cover with plastic wrap and refrigerate for at least 3 hours or overnight.

6. A few hours before serving, clean berries. Melt 6 oz (175 g) white chocolate over gently simmering water and dip strawberry ends into chocolate. Set strawberries on waxed paper-lined baking sheet to set. Reserve excess chocolate.

7. Very carefully, remove Charlotte from pan. Remove wrap. Mound strawberries inside edges of ladyfingers on top of mousse. Warm remaining melted white chocolate and drizzle over berries. Place extra berries around outside of charlotte. Dust everything with icing sugar.

A **Lighter Side:** Instead of the whipping cream, beat 4 egg whites until stiff peaks form. Fold into mousse base instead of the cream. Do not dip strawberries.

Manitou Coconut Mousse

*I*N *the summer of 1988 I started a cooking school program at the Inn and Tennis Club at Manitou in Ontario. The chef, Jean Pierre Challet, and the pastry chef, Jean Wolch, were both very talented. For one of our banquets, Jean Wolch prepared this sensational mousse.*

Although you could serve this with other fruit sauces, or even a chocolate sauce, the Passion Fruit Sauce on page 177 is Jean's recommendation, and is the perfect accompaniment because its tartness cuts the sweet taste and rich texture of the mousse.

Coconut cream is available in most specialty stores and supermarkets.

YIELD: Serves 8 to 10

1/4 cup	white rum	50 mL
1	envelope unflavored gelatin	1
1	355 mL tin cream of coconut, approx. 1-1/3 cups (325 mL)	1
2 cups	whipping cream	500 mL
2 tbsp	grated unsweetened coconut	25 mL
1/4 cup	shaved bittersweet or semisweet chocolate	50 mL

1. Place rum in small saucepan and sprinkle gelatin on top. Allow to rest for 5 minutes. Heat gently to dissolve gelatin.

2. In another saucepan, heat coconut cream. Whisk dissolved gelatin into coconut cream. Heat for 1 minute. Transfer to bowl and cool to room temperature.

3. Whip cream until light. Fold cream into cooled coconut base along with grated coconut.

4. Line the bottoms of eight custard cups with rounds of waxed or parchment paper. Pour in coconut mixture. Cover with plastic wrap and refrigerate for a few hours. To serve, run a knife around edge of mousses and unmold onto dessert plates. Sprinkle with shaved chocolate.

Hot Chocolate Soufflé with Quick Coffee Sauce

YIELD: Serves 6 to 8

*I*F *you want this soufflé to puff really high, use a 6 cup (1.5 L) soufflé dish; but if you want more crust (my favorite part), use the 8 cup (2 L) dish. If you are using the smaller pan, make a collar (see page 153).*

6 oz	bittersweet or semisweet chocolate, chopped	175 g
1/3 cup	unsalted butter	75 mL
6	egg yolks	6
8	egg whites	8
1/4 tsp	cream of tartar	1 mL
3 tbsp	granulated sugar	50 mL
2 cups	good-quality coffee ice cream	500 mL
	Sifted icing sugar	

1. Preheat oven to 450° F (220° C). Butter a 6 or 8 cup (1.5 or 2 L) soufflé dish with unsalted butter. Dust with sugar.

2. In the top of a double boiler, over gently simmering water, melt chocolate with butter.

3. Remove from heat and beat in egg yolks. Cool slightly while whisking.

4. In separate bowl, beat egg whites with cream of tartar until light. Beat in sugar, one tablespoon at a time, and beat until stiff.

5. Fold egg whites into soufflé base gently and spoon into prepared pan. Place pan in oven.

6. Reduce oven heat to 425° F (220° C) for 5 minutes. Reduce heat to 400° F (200° C) and continue baking for 20 to 25 minutes, or until very puffed.

7. While soufflé is baking, melt ice cream completely.

8. When soufflé is done, sprinkle with icing sugar and serve immediately. Spoon ice-cream sauce over the top.

A **Lighter Side:** Reduce butter by half. Serve with Raspberry Sauce (see page 179) instead of the coffee sauce.

Dark Chocolate Mousse in Double Chocolate Cups

*F*OR *these two-tone chocolate cups, line the muffin cups with dark chocolate; when that is set reline them with white chocolate. Be sure to use a fairly thick coating of chocolate each time, so that the difference in color is very clear.*

YIELD: Serves 12

	Double Chocolate Cups	
8 oz	bittersweet or semisweet chocolate	250 g
8 oz	white chocolate	250 g
	Dark Chocolate Mousse	
8 oz	bittersweet or semisweet chocolate	250 g
1/2 cup	unsalted butter, cut into cubes	125 mL
5	egg yolks	5
1/4 cup	raspberry or orange liqueur	50 mL
1 tsp	pure vanilla extract	5 mL
1-1/2 cups	whipping cream	375 mL
4 oz	bittersweet chocolate	125 g

1. In the top of a double boiler, over gently simmering water, melt dark chocolate and white chocolate, separately, until smooth. Allow chocolate to cool slightly.

2. With a small spoon or pastry brush, "paint" the inside of 12 large foil-lined muffin cups with dark chocolate. Chill or freeze until set. Repaint cups with the melted white chocolate. (If white chocolate has become too thick, warm slightly.) Chill or freeze again.

3. Working with one cup at a time, carefully remove paper, Reserve cups in refrigerator or freezer.

4. Prepare mousse by melting bittersweet chocolate in a double boiler over gently simmering water. Stir in butter until melted and smooth. Beat in egg yolks and continue to cook gently for a few minutes. Stir in liqueur and vanilla. Cool to room temperature.

5. In separate bowl, whip cream until light. Fold into chocolate base. Refrigerate mousse until it begins to firm up and hold its shape when mounded. Pipe or spoon attractively into chocolate cups. Eat extra mousse. Refrigerate cups.

6. With the remaining chocolate, shape curls, or melt chocolate and form into butterflies, leaves, etc. (see page 31). Decorate each mousse. Refrigerate until ready to serve.

A Lighter Side: Use 5 egg whites and fold into chocolate base in place of the whipping cream.

Buckwheat Crêpes with Caramelized Pears

YIELD: Serves 6
to 8

*W*HEN Bon Appetit *magazine wrote up the cooking school, we featured many delicious recipes. One of them was buckwheat crêpes filled with maple ice cream. I also prepare these "famous" crêpes with caramelized pears or apples. The combination of flavors is divine.*

	Crêpes	
4	eggs	4
2 tbsp	granulated sugar	25 mL
pinch	salt	pinch
1/2 cup	all-purpose flour	125 mL
1/2 cup	buckwheat flour	125 mL
3/4 cup	milk	175 mL
1/2 cup	water	125 mL
3 tbsp	unsalted butter, melted	50 mL
2 tbsp	unsalted butter	25 mL
	Filling	
10	ripe pears, preferably Bartlett	10
1 cup	granulated sugar	250 mL
1/3 cup	unsalted butter	75 mL
3/4 cup	whipping cream	175 mL

1. Prepare the crêpe batter by beating eggs together with sugar and salt in a large mixing bowl. Combine flours and whisk into the eggs. Slowly whisk in milk, water and melted butter. Allow batter to rest at room temperature for 1 hour (or longer in the refrigerator).

2. Heat an 8 inch (20 cm) crêpe or omelet pan. Add 2 tbsp (25 mL) unsalted butter and heat until sizzling stops. Add 1/4 cup (50 mL) batter to pan and swirl around pan to coat the bottom. Pour any excess batter back into the mixing bowl. Cook crêpe for 1 minute or until browned. Flip and cook second side for 30 to 60 seconds. (Second side never looks as good as the first side.) Continue until all batter is used. As the crêpes are finished, remove to a plate and stack them. They should keep in the refrigerator for 2 to 3 days and in the freezer for 1 month. (You should have 12 to 16 crêpes.)

3. Prepare filling by peeling pears. Cut them in half, remove cores and slice. Add sugar to a deep skillet. Cook over medium-high heat until sugar begins to brown. Add butter and allow butter to melt. Do not worry if sugar crystallizes a little. Add pears and cook, partially covered, for 30 to 40 minutes, or until tender.

4. Remove pears with a slotted spoon and reserve. Add cream to juices remaining in pan. Bring to a boil and reduce to a thin sauce consistency.

5. To assemble crêpes, place the 12 best ones, nicest side up, on a work surface. Divide pears among crêpes. Roll up and place in individual ovenproof oval dishes or on a baking sheet. Just before serving, warm for 5 to 10 minutes in a preheated 350° F (180° C) oven. Rewarm sauce if necessary. Spoon sauce over warm crêpes. Serve with vanilla, cinnamon or caramel ice cream if desired.

A Lighter Side: Omit the whipping cream from the filling. Make only half the pear mixture.

Cappuccino Mousse

*Y*OU *can pipe this mousse into chocolate cups (see page 121), cookie cups (see page 122), or you can serve it in coffee mugs with a little whipped cream on top, dusted with cocoa or sprinkled with coffee bean-shaped chocolates.*

YIELD: Serves 8 to 10

1/2 cup	extra-strong coffee	125 mL
1	envelope unflavored gelatin	1
3	egg yolks	3
1/2 cup	icing sugar	125 mL
3 tbsp	coffee liqueur	50 mL
1 tsp	pure vanilla extract	5 mL
2 cups	whipping cream	500 mL

1. Place coffee in small saucepan and sprinkle with gelatin. Allow to rest for 5 minutes. Heat gently to dissolve.

2. In separate saucepan, beat egg yolks with icing sugar until thick and creamy. Blend in gelatin mixture and liqueur. Cook gently, stirring constantly, until mixture thickens, about 2 to 5 minutes. Stir in vanilla. Cool to room temperature.

3. Whip cream until light. Stir one-third cream into coffee base to lighten. Then fold in remaining cream gently.

A Lighter Side: Beat 5 egg whites with an extra 1/3 cup (75 mL) granulated sugar until stiff. Use instead of the whipping cream.

Profiteroles with Ice Cream, Raspberry and Chocolate Sauce

YIELD: 24 small puffs

*P*ROFITEROLES *are crusty little containers for ice cream or pastry cream. The same dough can be used to make eclairs, croquembouche and gâteau St. Honoré. The profiteroles can be made ahead and frozen. If you are filling them with ice cream, you can freeze them filled. That way the dessert is very easy to assemble. For this recipe, swirl the two sauces on the plate attractively. If you are making concentric circles, fill two plastic squeeze bottles with the sauce for easy handling. You can also just spoon one sauce on one side of the plate, the other on the second side, and allow them to swirl together in the center.*

1 cup	water	250 mL
1/4 cup	unsalted butter	50 mL
1/4 tsp	salt	1 mL
2 tbsp	granulated sugar	25 mL
1 cup	all-purpose flour	250 mL
4	eggs	4
	Glaze	
1	egg	1
1 tbsp	cream	15 mL
	Filling	
2 cups	good-quality vanilla ice cream	500 mL
	Sauce	
1	recipe Raspberry Sauce (page 179)	1
1	recipe Dark Chocolate Sauce (page 185)	1
	Sifted icing sugar	

1. Place water in a heavy saucepan. Cut butter into bits and add to water with salt and sugar. Bring to a boil.

2. Remove from heat and stir in flour all at once. Stir until mixture comes away from sides of pan and forms a ball.

3. Return to heat. Smear mixture repeatedly along bottom of pan until it dries and slightly coats pan. Transfer dough to a bowl and cool for about 5 minutes.

4. Beat in eggs one at a time. Mixture will be slippery but will come together in the end.

5. Preheat oven to 425° F (220° C). Line baking sheets with parchment paper. Spoon or pipe dough in 24 mounds on cookie sheet.

6. To make glaze, beat egg with cream and brush tops of puffs. Bake for 5 minutes. Reduce heat to 375° F (190° C). Bake for 25 to 20 minutes longer for small puffs. Cool.

7. To serve, cut off tops and scoop out any unbaked centers. Fill with ice cream and freeze. Replace tops if you wish.

8. Serve two or three profiteroles per person. Swirl sauces on large white dinner plates as suggested above. Set profiteroles on top. Dust with icing sugar.

A **Lighter Side:** Fill profiteroles with a sorbet instead of ice cream, and serve with just the raspberry sauce.

Soufflé Crêpes with Cointreau Flambé

*A*LTHOUGH *this dessert is not very rich, it certainly seems extravagant. Light, dreamy pillows of a flavorful orange soufflé are surrounded by a tender crêpe drenched in Cointreau. The crêpes can be made a day or two ahead, but the whole thing should be assembled a few hours before dinner. You do have to bake and flambé them just before serving.*

	Crêpes	
4	eggs	4
1 cup	all-purpose flour	250 mL
1/4 cup	granulated sugar	50 mL
pinch	salt	pinch
1 cup	milk	250 mL
1/3 cup	water	75 mL
1 tsp	finely grated orange peel	5 mL
2 tbsp	unsalted butter, melted	25 mL
	Soufflé	
1/4 cup	cornstarch	50 mL
1/2 cup	granulated sugar, divided	125 mL
1 cup	milk, cold	250 mL
3	eggs, separated	3
1/4 cup	Cointreau or other orange liqueur	50 mL
pinch	cream of tartar	pinch
	Flambé	
1/4 cup	Cointreau or other orange liqueur	50 mL
2 tbsp	Cognac or brandy	25 mL
1/4 cup	icing sugar, sifted	50 mL

1. Prepare crêpe batter by whisking eggs with flour, sugar and salt. Carefully beat in milk, water, peel and melted butter. Cover bowl and allow batter to rest at room temperature for 1 hour.

2. To prepare crêpes, heat another tablespoon of unsalted butter in an 8 inch (20 cm) crêpe or omelet pan. Add a ladleful of batter to the pan. Swirl batter to coat the bottom of pan and pour any excess batter back into the bowl. Cook the crêpe until brown and then flip. Cook second side. Remove from pan. Repeat until all the batter has been used. You should have 12 to 16 crêpes. Crêpes can be stacked on top of each other. Cover and refrigerate until ready to use.

3. For the soufflé, combine cornstarch, 1/3 cup (75 mL) sugar and cold milk in medium saucepan. Whisk until smooth. Cook gently until mixture thickens and just comes to a boil, stirring constantly.

4. Beat egg yolks in a small bowl. Beat in a little of the hot custard.

5. Beat yolk mixture back into the rest of the sauce and stir in the liqueur. Transfer mixture to large bowl.

6. In separate bowl, beat egg whites with cream of tartar until light. Slowly beat in remaining sugar. Beat until firm. Stir a little of the whites into egg-yolk sauce to lighten and then fold remaining whites in gently.

7. Preheat over to 425° F (220° C). Butter a large shallow baking dish (or two smaller ones).

8. To assemble, arrange crêpes, "bad" (second cooked side) up, on a counter. Spoon a little of the soufflé mixture along one end of the crêpe. Fold into thirds or roll up very gently, to give soufflé a little room to expand. Arrange crêpes in a buttered shallow casserole dish.

9. Bake crêpes for 10 to 12 minutes, or until well puffed.

10. Warm Cointreau and Cognac in a small saucepan. When crêpes come out of the oven, dust them with icing sugar. Ignite the liqueurs and pour over crêpes (see page 26).

Crème Caramel

YIELD: Serves 8 to 10

T HERE was a time when I thought I would never taste anything that was too rich for me. I've also always loved the taste and texture of dairy products. So a dessert like this one was always my ideal.

I gradually came to be more careful about foods high in fat, but I still adore this dessert, no matter how much I try not to. And when I want real comfort, this is where I turn with my spoon.

This dessert really needs no garnish, although a strawberry or edible flower would be nice if you think the plate looks a little bare.

	Caramel	
1 cup	granulated sugar	250 mL
1/4 cup	water	50 mL
	Custard	
6	egg yolks	6
1/3 cup	granulated sugar	75 mL
1-1/4 cups	light cream, hot	300 mL
1 cup	whipping cream, hot	250 mL
2 tsp	pure vanilla extract	10 mL

1. Preheat oven to 325° F (160° C).

2. To make caramel, combine sugar with water in medium heavy saucepan. Stir over medium heat until sugar has dissolved. Without stirring, cook on medium-high until mixture turns a golden caramel color. Occasionally brush down any sugar crystals clinging to sides of pan with a brush dipped in cold water. Pour caramel into 8 or 10 small ramekins.

3. To make custard, in large bowl, beat egg yolks with sugar. Whisk in hot light cream and whipping cream. Stir in vanilla. Strain mixture and discard any froth that has formed on the surface. Divide mixture between caramel-lined dishes.

4. Place ramekins in water bath (see page 9) with hot water coming halfway up sides of pan. Bake for 25 to 30 minutes, or until set. Chill for 3 hours.

5. Unmold by running a small thin knife around inside edge of pans. Invert onto serving plates. Spoon out extra caramel and pour over.

A Lighter Side: Use three whole eggs and two egg yolks. Use milk instead of whipping cream. (You could also make this with four whole eggs and milk instead of the light cream and whipping cream, but the texture won't be nearly as smooth.)

Coffee Crème Brûlée

CRÈME *brûlée now has almost a cult following; devotees endlessly discuss which kind of sugar to use on the top (brown), when to broil it (close to serving time), how much to serve (small portions), and what temperature to serve it at (really cold). The thing no one should ever discuss is the number of calories! If you prefer a plain version, just leave out the coffee.*

YIELD: Serves 8

3 cups	whipping cream	750 mL
2 tbsp	instant coffee powder	25 mL
1	vanilla bean, cut into 6 pieces, or 2 tsp (10 mL) pure vanilla extract	1
8	egg yolks	8
1/3 cup	granulated sugar	75 mL
1 cup	brown sugar	250 mL

1. Preheat oven to 350° F (180° C).

2. Place whipping cream, coffee and vanilla bean in heavy saucepan. (If using vanilla extract, add it to the custard later.) Bring to a boil on medium heat. Turn off heat. Stir to dissolve coffee powder. Remove vanilla bean. (Rinse and dry it and store it in your sugar canister.)

3. In large bowl, beat egg yolks with granulated sugar until light and lemony. Slowly whisk in coffee-flavored cream. (Add vanilla now if you are using it.)

4. Divide mixture among 8 small ramekins. Place ramekins in water bath (see page 9).

5. Bake for 35 to 40 minutes, or until set. Remove from water bath, cool and chill in the refrigerator for 6 hours or overnight.

6. A few hours before serving, press brown sugar through strainer to make sure it is absolutely smooth. Divide sugar among the custards and press gently to spread sugar evenly over surface.

7. Preheat boiler. Place custards on a baking sheet. Broil about 6 inches (15 cm) from the element until sugar melts. It should look like a sheet of ice. The sugar will probably blacken in spots — just don't let it burn too much. Chill until ready to serve. (If the sugar is melted too far in advance, sometimes it liquefies before you get a chance to serve it. The dessert is still delicious, but doesn't have the marvelous characteristic crunch.)

A Lighter Side: Use light cream, or even milk, in place of the whipping cream. Use 4 whole eggs and 2 egg yolks in place of the 8 egg yolks.

Amaretti Caramel Custard

YIELD: Serves 8
to 10

*B*EING *so fond of caramel, I am always on the lookout for new caramel recipes. The idea for this one came from the celebrated Italian cook, teacher and author, Marcella Hazan. It has the traditional caramel coating for a crème caramel, but the custard is flavored with chocolate and amaretti biscuits. I usually prepare it in a ring mold and then fill the center with whipped cream and strawberries, but it can also be made in a soufflé dish with the cream and berries surrounding it. Make sure the serving dish has a slight lip, to catch every drop of the caramel.*

	Caramel	
3/4 cup	granulated sugar	175 mL
3 tbsp	water	50 mL
	Custard	
6 oz	amaretti biscuits	175 g
3 oz	bittersweet or semisweet chocolate	90 g
1 cup	whipping cream	250 mL
2 cups	milk	500 mL
4	eggs	4
3	egg yolks	3
1/2 cup	granulated sugar	125 mL
3 tbsp	dark rum	50 mL
	Garnish	
1 cup	whipping cream	250 mL
2 cups	strawberries	500 mL

1. Preheat oven to 350° F (180° C).

2. For the caramel, combine sugar with water in a medium heavy saucepan. Cook, stirring, until sugar dissolves. Continue cooking, without stirring, until caramel turns a deep golden-brown. Carefully pour caramel into a ring mold and rotate pan (using potholders) until caramel coats pan.

3. To make custard, chop amaretti and chocolate until fine. A food processor works well for this. Place in large bowl.

4. Heat cream and milk and pour over amaretti mixture. Allow to stand for 5 to 10 minutes. Stir; chocolate should be melted and amaretti should be softened.

5. Beat eggs with yolks and sugar until light and lemony. Beat into milk mixture with rum. Pour into caramel-lined pan.

6. Bake in a water bath (see page 9) for 40 to 45 minutes, or until custard has set. Cool and then chill.

7. To unmold, sit pan in hot water for a minute to dissolve caramel. Unmold onto a dish with a small lip to catch the caramel sauce. (If all the caramel has not come away from the mold, warm it further in a dish of hot water or place it briefly in a hot oven.)

8. For garnish, whip cream until light. Hull berries and halve them. Place cream in the center of custard, with berries around the outside edge.

A Lighter Side: Use all milk instead of the cream, and one additional whole egg in place of the 3 yolks.

Mascarpone Torta with Figs and Walnuts

*W*HEN *you want dessert but don't want dessert, this sophisticated dish fits the bill. Serve it on crackers or brioche. If you cannot find mascarpone, use 12 oz (375 g) cream cheese or chèvre mixed with 1/2 cup (125 mL) unsalted butter instead. If you cannot find fresh figs for the garnish, use sliced kiwi fruit and black grapes.*

YIELD: Serves 8 to 10

1 lb	mascarpone cheese	500 g
8 oz	cream cheese, firm	250 g
8 oz	dried figs	250 g
1/2 cup	dry port	125 mL
3/4 cup	toasted walnuts	175 mL
	Garnish	
5	fresh figs	5
8	walnut halves	8
	Fresh basil or mint	

1. In large bowl, cream mascarpone with cream cheese until smooth.

2. Cut dried figs into very small pieces (scissors work well) and cook with port in small saucepan until mixture is jam-like, about 15 minutes.

3. Combine walnuts and fig mixture.

4. Line a soufflé dish, charlotte mold or brioche pan with plastic wrap. Spoon in a layer of cheese. Spread with a layer of figs and repeat layers, ending with cheese. (If fig mixture is too stiff to spread, warm it slightly.) Wrap well and refrigerate overnight.

5. Unmold onto serving plate. Cut fresh figs into wedges. Garnish torta with figs, walnut halves and greens.

The Ultimate Bread Pudding

*B*READ *pudding was originally devised to use up leftovers. But this version defies its origins. Rich with egg yolks and cream, it contains brioche, which lightens the dish and helps to give it its ethereal texture. When baked, the bread floats on top of a smooth, silky custard.*

1 cup	boiling water	250 mL
1/3 cup	raisins	75 mL
1-1/2 cups	whipping cream	375 mL
1-1/2 cups	light cream	375 mL
8	egg yolks	8
1/2 cup	granulated sugar	125 mL
2 tsp	pure vanilla extract	10 mL
4 oz	brioche rolls or loaf, thinly sliced, or other rich egg bread	125 g
3 tbsp	unsalted butter	50 mL
3 tbsp	apricot jam	50 mL

1. Preheat oven to 350° F (180° C). Butter an 8 inch (2 L) baking dish.

2. Pour boiling water over raisins and allow to soak for 10 minutes. Drain well.

3. Meanwhile, place both kinds of cream in a saucepan and heat gently.

4. In a bowl, beat egg yolks with sugar. Beat in cream and vanilla. Strain mixture. (Vanilla beans can be rinsed, dried and stored in your sugar canister.)

5. Sprinkle half of the raisins in bottom of baking dish. Butter brioche and arrange buttered side up in the dish in a single layer or slightly overlapping. Sprinkle with remaining raisins. Pour in custard.

6. Bake in a water bath (see page 9) for 50 to 60 minutes, or until just set. Cool for about 15 minutes.

7. Heat jam and brush over top of pudding. Serve warm or cold.

A Lighter Side: Use milk instead of the light cream and whipping cream. Use 5 whole eggs instead of 8 egg yolks. Of course, this version will not be as rich as the original, but it will still work.

Tiramisu with Zabaione

YIELD: Serves 8 to 10

*T*IRAMISU *seems to be the carrot cake of the eighties. Soft and creamy, tender and luscious, and with that name ("lift me up") it can hardly miss.*

Of all the variations I have tried, this is my favorite. It's a little extra work because you do have to cook the custard (zabaione), but the effort, I feel, brings even greater rewards.

Raffaello Ferrari, the talented chef at Centro (one of Toronto's hottest restaurants) showed me a stunning way to serve this. Place a square of the tiramisu on one side of a dinner plate. Place a spoon and fork, crisscrossed, beside it. Through a sieve, dust cocoa all over the plate, spoon and fork. Very carefully, without disturbing the cocoa, remove the spoon and fork. The outline of the cutlery should remain.

Do try to find the mascarpone cheese called for in the recipe. It is very special. (Be sure to buy "mascarpone" and not "torta," which is a combination of mascarpone and gorgonzola — not good for this recipe at all.) If you cannot find it, use half cream cheese and half ricotta.

Make the ladyfingers (see page 110) and dry them on racks overnight before using, or buy the dry Italian ladyfingers.

6	eggs, separated	6
1/3 cup	granulated sugar	75 mL
1/2 cup	Cognac, divided	125 mL
1/2 cup	dry Marsala wine, divided	125 mL
1 lb	mascarpone cheese	500 g
20	ladyfingers, dry	20
1/2 cup	extra-strong coffee	125 mL
6 oz	bittersweet or semisweet chocolate, chopped	175 g

1. Beat egg yolks with sugar until light and lemony. Beat in 1/4 cup (50 mL) each Cognac and Marsala. Cook over gently simmering water until thickened. Cool.

2. In large bowl, beat mascarpone until smooth. Beat in cooled custard.

3. Whip egg whites until light and firm and fold into zabaione mixture.

4. Arrange half of the ladyfingers in the bottom of a 12 cup (3 L) shallow bowl. Combine coffee with remaining Cognac and Marsala and sprinkle half of it over the ladyfingers. Spread with half the cream. Repeat layers.

5. Sprinkle the top with chocolate. Wrap with plastic and refrigerate overnight.

A Lighter Side: Omit egg yolks and do not make the custard. Beat the mascarpone with the sugar and liqueurs. Fold in the beaten egg whites.

Coronets with Pastry Cream and Berry Berry Sauce

YIELD: Serves 8

*T*HIS *dessert is breathtaking to behold, and so incredibly delicious that even if nothing else in the meal worked, guests would walk away from your house on a cloud after eating this. This dessert truly is, as they say, "to die for." It seems long and complicated, but because everything except the assembly can be done ahead, it really isn't hard at all.*

The fruit in the sauce should be fresh. If you cannot find fresh raspberries and blueberries, use more strawberries. You can also double the fruit in the sauce recipe and serve it alone as a fruit salad.

1/2 cup	granulated sugar	125 mL
1/3 cup	all-purpose flour	75 mL
2	egg whites	2
1/4 cup	unsalted butter, melted	50 mL
2 tsp	water	10 mL
1 tsp	pure vanilla extract	5 mL
	Pastry Cream	
1 cup	milk	250 mL
3	egg yolks	3
1/3 cup	granulated sugar	75 mL
3 tbsp	all-purpose flour	50 mL
3/4 cup	whipping cream	175 mL
1 tsp	pure vanilla extract	5 mL
3 tbsp	orange liqueur	50 mL
	Berry Berry Sauce	
1	10 oz (300 g) package frozen raspberries	1
2 tbsp	orange or raspberry liqueur	25 mL
2 cups	fresh strawberries, hulled and cut into quarters	500 mL
1 cup	fresh raspberries	250 mL
1 cup	fresh blueberries	250 mL
	Sifted icing sugar	

1. Preheat oven to 400° F (200° C). Butter and lightly flour two rimless baking sheets. Press a 2-1/2 inch (6 cm) round cookie cutter into the flour/butter coating to trace twelve outlines on each baking sheet.

2. To prepare coronets, combine granulated sugar, flour, egg whites, melted butter, water and vanilla.

3. Place a tablespoon of batter in each of three rounds and spread batter to fill rounds.

4. Bake for 5 to 6 minutes, or until cookies are browned around the edges. Remove from cookie sheets and shape into small coronets while cookies are hot. Repeat until all the batter is used. You should have 24 small coronets. These can be made ahead and frozen in a sturdy container.

5. To prepare pastry cream, heat milk in medium saucepan.

6. In bowl, beat egg yolks with sugar until lemony and then beat in flour. Whisk in hot milk and return to saucepan. Bring to boil. Cook, stirring, for a few minutes. Custard will be very thick. Transfer mixture to large bowl. Cool.

7. In separate bowl, whip cream with vanilla and liqueur until stiff. Fold into custard. (This can be done up to 8 hours ahead of time.) Refrigerate.

8. For the sauce, defrost berries and strain. Reserve juices. Puree berries through a food mill to remove seeds. (Or puree in a blender or food processor and then strain.) Add enough reserved juices to make a medium-thick sauce. Add liqueur. Gently stir in strawberries, raspberries and blueberries.

9. Assemble dessert just before serving. Place pastry cream in a piping tube and fill coronets. Place three coronets on individual dinner-sized plates at 12, 4 and 8 o'clock. Spoon sauce in between. Dust the coronets, berries and plate with icing sugar.

A Lighter Side: Use lightly sweetened plain yogurt or light sour cream instead of the filling.

Rice Pudding with Dried Fruit

YIELD: Serves 6 to 8

*E*VEN *though I make many fancy, gorgeous desserts, rice pudding is possibly my all-time favorite. It's warm and comfortable, cozy and creamy. Without the dried fruit, this is my classic recipe but, always wanting to surge forward, I now make it with flavorful apricots and prunes in addition to the mandatory raisins. Try to find short-grain rice; it will give you much creamier results.*

1/2 cup	short-grain rice	125 mL
1 cup	boiling water	250 mL
1/3 cup	granulated sugar	75 mL
1 tsp	cornstarch	5 mL
pinch	salt	pinch
4 cups	milk	1 L
1 cup	light cream	250 mL
pinch	ground nutmeg	pinch
1/3 cup	raisins	75 mL
1/3 cup	diced dried apricots	75 mL
1/3 cup	diced pitted prunes	75 mL
2	egg yolks, optional	2
1 tsp	pure vanilla extract	5 mL
1 tbsp	ground cinnamon	15 mL

1. Combine rice with boiling water in a large saucepan. Cover. Simmer gently for 15 minutes, or until water is absorbed.

2. Combine sugar with cornstarch and salt. Whisk in 1 cup (250 mL) milk. Stir until smooth. Add sugar mixture along with remaining milk and cream to the saucepan with the rice. Combine well. Add nutmeg and raisins. Stirring, bring to a boil. Cover, reduce heat to the barest simmer and cook for 30 minutes.

3. Add apricots and prunes and continue to cook very gently, covered, stirring every 5 to 10 minutes, until mixture is very creamy and thick. This will take approximately 30 to 45 minutes.

4. If you are using egg yolks, beat them in a small bowl. Whisk in a little of the pudding and then add yolk mixture back to rest of pudding. Remove from heat. Stir in vanilla.

5. Transfer to an attractive serving bowl or six to eight individual bowls. Sprinkle top with cinnamon. Serve warm or cold.

A **Lighter Side:** Omit the cream and egg yolks. Use 2 percent milk.

8

Sauces

DESSERT sauces have become very fashionable. Even when a restaurant serves a home-style dessert like bread pudding or apple crisp, they usually dress it up (whether it needs it or not) with a drizzle of sauce under or over it. A dessert served with a sauce usually does look prettier, though, and it is so easy that you should consider this extra touch when you are entertaining. Good-quality store-bought ice cream or sorbets can look like a million dollars scooped in ovals and served on a bed of three different-colored fruit sauces swirled together in a gorgeous design.

Many times, of course, a dessert does taste better with a sauce. Cakes with dry textures can be moistened with sauces; sauces also can complement flavors. Not only does a coffee sauce on a chocolate pâté cut the intensity and the dense texture of the chocolate, but who can resist the combination of flavors?

The sauces in this chapter are all pretty easy, and there are also many other sauces with other recipes in the book (check the index under sauces for a listing of them). Mix and match the flavors you like.

Here are a few helpful hints about sauces. There are many more included in the actual recipes.

Sauce Tips

• Sometimes recipes instruct you to cook sauces in a double boiler. (For information about double boilers, see page 11.) This is usually because the sauce is delicate (it may contain egg yolks) and could curdle easily. If you choose not to use a double boiler, cook the sauce in a heavy-bottomed pot on very gentle heat and stir constantly. Be very careful not to overcook.

• Add egg yolks to a hot sauce carefully. Egg yolks demand respect, since they can curdle easily. Always beat the yolks together lightly and add a little of the hot sauce to the egg yolks first. Then, off the heat, add these slightly warmed egg yolks to the pot of sauce. Whisk together and cook gently, stirring constantly until just thickened. (If you just dump the cold yolks into the hot sauce they may have a nervous breakdown and curdle!)

• If a sauce contains a starch such as flour or cornstarch and eggs, the sauce should be brought to a boil. The eggs will not curdle. When it comes to a boil, reduce or turn off the heat as the recipe instructs. If there is no starch in a sauce containing egg yolks, the sauce will usually curdle if it reaches a boil. As soon as the first bubble appears through the surface, whisk to cool the sauce and remove it from the heat.

• As an extra precaution, when making a sauce (especially if it contains egg yolks), have an empty mixing bowl close to the stove. If you feel the sauce is too hot, transfer it to the cool bowl immediately and stir like mad. Taking a saucepan off the heat does not stop the cooking completely because of the heat that remains in the pan itself. Another trick is to remove the pan from the heat and add an ice cube to the sauce, which will also lower the temperature quickly. Sometimes, however, you do not want a few spoonfuls of water in your sauce.

• If you want to cool a sauce, it is a good idea to transfer it to a bowl or cool saucepan. If you really want it to cool quickly, set the bowl over a larger bowl of ice mixed with cold water. Stir often and the sauce will cool much more quickly than it would if you put it in the refrigerator.

• When you are cooling a sauce and do not want a skin to form on the surface, simply place a piece of plastic wrap directly on the surface of the sauce.

• Cooked sauces usually thicken a little on cooling. If necessary, adjust the consistency with a little milk, cream, fruit juice or water when you rewarm them.

Passion Fruit Sauce

*T*HIS *sauce is from Jean Wolch, pastry chef at the luxurious Ontario resort, the Inn at Manitou. It can be served with many desserts, but it is perfect with his Coconut Mousse (see page 157). If you find the sauce too tart, add extra sugar.*

Passion fruit nectar (sometimes called pulp or juice) is available at health food stores.

YIELD:
Approximately 2 cups (500 mL)

1-1/2 cups	passion fruit nectar	375 mL
1/2 cup	orange juice	125 mL
2 tbsp	lime juice	25 mL
1/2 cup	granulated sugar	125 mL

1. In a small or medium saucepan, heat passion fruit nectar with orange juice, lime juice and sugar. Cook for 3 minutes. Cool.

Maple Rum Cream Sauce

*T*HIS *sauce is so wonderful with apple cobbler and apple crisp! But it also tastes great with chocolate cake or over ice cream. Instead of rum you can use brandy or orange liqueur, or you can omit the liqueur entirely.*

YIELD:
Approximately 1-1/2 cups (375 mL)

1 cup	pure maple syrup	250 mL
3 tbsp	dark rum	50 mL
3/4 cup	whipping cream	175 mL
1 tbsp	unsalted butter	15 mL
1/2 tsp	pure vanilla extract	2 mL

1. Bring syrup and rum to a boil. Cook over medium heat for 5 minutes.

2. Standing back in case mixture bubbles up, add cream. Cook gently 2 minutes longer.

3. Remove from heat and stir in butter and vanilla.

Caramel Sauce

YIELD:
Approximately
1-1/2 cups (375 mL)

*W*HENEVER *I want a fast dessert that tastes like a million dollars, I make this caramel sauce and serve it over really good-quality coffee or vanilla ice cream. For a great presentation, drizzle sauce over individual serving plates, place three oval scoops of ice cream (radiating out from the center) on top and then scatter fresh raspberries, blueberries or strawberries over the entire thing!*

1 cup	granulated sugar	250 mL
3 tbsp	water	50 mL
3/4 cup	whipping cream	175 mL

1. Place sugar and water in a medium or large heavy saucepan. Cook, stirring constantly, until sugar dissolves.

2. Stop stirring and cook until sugar turns a deep caramel color. Have a bowl of cold water and pastry brush close by. Dip brush in water and brush any sugar crystals from the sides of the pan back down into the liquid sugar mixture. Be careful not to burn the caramel. (If you do, start again.) If the sugar crystallizes before turning to caramel, you can add a little more water and continue cooking until crystals melt, or you can begin again.

3. Remove pan from heat and, very carefully (averting your face and standing back), add cream. Continue to cook and stir until sauce is smooth.

4. Serve warm or at room temperature. Sauce will thicken when cold — warm up gently to serve.

A **Lighter Side:** Use light cream instead of whipping cream.

Pecan Caramel Sauce

YIELD:
Approximately
1-1/2 cups (375 mL)

I was going to add this as a variation to the caramel sauce, but I was afraid that people might overlook it! Serve over ice cream or bread pudding.

1 cup	granulated sugar	250 mL
3 tbsp	water	50 mL
3/4 cup	whipping cream	175 mL
2 tbsp	unsalted butter	25 mL
3/4 cup	pecans, toasted (whole or chopped)	175 mL
2 tbsp	Bourbon or Scotch	25 mL

1. Place sugar and water in a medium or large heavy saucepan. Cook, stirring constantly, until sugar dissolves.

2. Stop stirring and cook until sugar turns a deep caramel color. Have a bowl of cold water and a pastry brush close by. Dip brush in water and brush any sugar crystals from the sides of the pan back down into the liquid sugar mixture. Be careful not to burn the caramel. (If you do, start again.) If the sugar crystallizes before turning to caramel, you can add a little more water and continue cooking until crystals melt, or you can begin again.

3. Remove pan from heat and, very carefully (averting your face and standing back), add cream. Continue to cook and stir until sauce is smooth. Stir in butter, pecans and Bourbon.

4. Serve warm or at room temperature. Sauce will thicken when cold — warm up gently to serve.

A Lighter Side: Use light cream instead of whipping cream, and omit butter.

Raspberry Sauce

*T*HIS *is the most wonderful dessert sauce. It can be used on ice creams, sorbets, sponge or angel food cakes as well as chocolate cakes, mousses and fruit. Definitely all-purpose!*

For an extraordinary flavor in the sauce, use Chambord, a raspberry-fla-vored liqueur. It is conveniently available in tiny liqueur bottles. An orange liqueur can be used instead.

YIELD:
Approximately
1-1/2 cups (375 mL)

1	10 oz (300 g) package frozen raspberries, or 2 cups (500 mL) fresh raspberries	1
2 tbsp	fruit sugar, approx.	25 mL
2 tbsp	raspberry jam	25 mL
2 tbsp	raspberry liqueur	25 mL

1. Defrost raspberries and drain, reserving juice.

2. Puree berries with fruit sugar and jam. (If you puree berries in a food mill, it will puree and strain out the seeds. If you use a blender or a food processor, strain the mixture after pureeing to remove seeds.)

3. Stir in liqueur. Adjust thickness with reserved juice. (If you are using fresh berries, thin sauce with orange juice if necessary.) Add more sugar to taste if desired.

Rum Raisin Sauce

YIELD:
Approximately
1-1/2 cups (375 mL)

INSTEAD of being addicted to rum raisin ice cream, become attached to this sauce. It is superb over vanilla ice cream, or you could make yourself a double hit sundae and serve it over rum raisin ice cream. It's also great on bread pudding.

1 cup	raisins	250 mL
2 cups	boiling water	500 mL
1 cup	granulated sugar	250 mL
3 tbsp	water	50 mL
3/4 cup	whipping cream	175 mL
1/4 cup	dark rum	50 mL

1. Soak raisins in boiling water for 15 minutes. Drain well and discard water.

2. Place sugar and water in a medium or large heavy saucepan. Cook, stirring constantly, until sugar dissolves.

3. Stop stirring and cook until sugar turns a deep caramel color. Have a bowl of cold water and pastry brush close by. Dip brush in water and brush any sugar crystals from the sides of the pan back down into the liquid sugar mixture. Be careful not to burn the caramel. (If you do, start again.) If the sugar crystallizes before turning to caramel, you can add a little more water and continue cooking until crystals melt, or you can begin again.

4. Remove pan from heat and, very carefully (averting your face and standing back), add cream. Continue to cook and stir until sauce is smooth. Add raisins and rum.

5. Serve warm or at room temperature. Sauce will thicken when cold — warm up gently to serve.

A **Lighter Side:** Use light cream instead of whipping cream.

Apricot Mango Sauce

*M*ANGOES *have become very popular in the past few years. For best results, be sure the mangoes are ripe — otherwise the flavor can be less than exotic.*

This sauce is terrific with chocolate desserts or with anything lemony or coconut. I like to swirl mango, kiwi and raspberry sauces on a dessert plate and then arrange scoops of chocolate mousse or sorbets on top. It looks stunning, with a taste to match.

YIELD:
Approximately
1-1/2 cups (375 mL)

2	ripe mangoes	2
2 tbsp	apricot liqueur or orange liqueur, or frozen orange juice concentrate	25 mL
2 tbsp	apricot jam	25 mL

1. Peel mangoes and dice.

2. Puree mango fruit with liqueur and jam. Thin with orange juice if necessary.

Rum Kiwi Sauce

*K*IWIS *are a beautiful fruit that add color and flavor to fruit salads, fruit flans and sorbets (though I have never been a fan of kiwis with chicken or shrimp!).*

This sauce tastes great and looks lovely. You can swirl it on a dessert plate with mango and raspberry sauce, or serve it plain over lemon or coconut sorbets. It is also a stunning sauce for any lemon dessert or cheesecake.

YIELD:
Approximately 1 cup
(250 mL)

4	kiwi fruit	4
1 tbsp	dark rum	15 mL
1 tsp	lemon juice	5 mL
3 tbsp	granulated sugar	50 mL
2 tbsp	water	25 mL

1. Peel kiwi fruit by cutting a small piece off the top and bottom. Stand fruit up on cutting surface and cut off skin from top to bottom.

2. Cut fruit into small pieces and puree in a blender or food processor.

3. Place rum, lemon juice, sugar and water in a small saucepan and bring to a boil. Add to kiwi fruit and puree.

Chantilly Cream
(Whipped Cream)

YIELD:
Approximately 1 cup
(250 mL)

O NCE when I first began teaching, a student told me that a recipe she'd seen in a magazine was too complicated for her because it called for Chantilly cream. When I told her Chantilly cream was just whipped cream with a little sugar and vanilla, she thought I was kidding. Then I started to wonder. I was right, but even I almost got psyched out by a sophisticated name!

Anyway, here are three whipped cream recipes. One is plain, one is chocolate and one is caramel. They are all delicious and easy to make. They can be served with a dessert or used as an icing for a cake.

When I add sugar to whipped cream, I usually use icing sugar, as the cream seems to keep better. Icing sugar also contains cornstarch and adds a little body to the cream. Don't use too much, though, or you may start to taste the cornstarch in the icing sugar.

If you are beating cream to fold into a dessert, do not beat it too stiff. By the time you have folded it and stirred it into other ingredients, it could become overbeaten and slightly buttery in taste and texture. If you are using the cream as a garnish, beat it a little more, but be aware that when you put it into a piping tube, you are also handling it a little more, so be careful. If you overbeat cream and it does turn to butter, do not throw it away. Try adding a little more unwhipped cream, and beat again until whipped properly. If this doesn't work, continue to beat, squeeze out any excess water, and use it as butter (if it is unflavored), or in baking if you have already added sugar.

1 cup	whipping cream	250 mL
1 tbsp	icing sugar, sifted	15 mL
1 tbsp	liqueur, optional	15 mL
1/2 tsp	pure vanilla extract	2 mL

1. Make sure cream, beaters and bowl are very cold.

2. Whip cream until light. Add sugar, liqueur (if using) and vanilla. Continue to beat until desired thickness.

Chocolate Whipped Cream

*T*HIS *can be used as a quick chocolate mousse as well as a garnish or icing. Once it is refrigerated, though, it tends to firm up as the chocolate sets. So use it immediately if you intend to pipe or spread it.*

YIELD:
Approximately 1 cup
(250 mL)

1 cup	whipping cream, divided	250 mL
3 oz	bittersweet or semisweet chocolate, chopped	90 g
1 tbsp	liqueur, optional	15 mL

1. Heat 1/2 cup (125 mL) cream until it just comes to the boil. Pour it over the chopped chocolate. Allow mixture to rest for 2 or 3 minutes and then stir to melt chocolate. Stir until smooth. (If the chocolate is not smooth and completely melted, heat gently over hot water until it is.)

2. Stir in remaining cream and liqueur. Chill until cool to the touch.

3. Beat cream, watching carefully, until soft peaks form. Use as needed.

Caramel Whipped Cream

*T*HIS *is really different and wonderful. Serve it with chocolate desserts, fruit desserts — with anything!*

YIELD:
Approximately
2 cups (500 mL)

1/2 cup	granulated sugar	125 mL
2 tbsp	water	25 mL
1/4 cup	boiling water	50 mL
2 cups	whipping cream	500 mL

1. Make caramel by combining sugar with water in a medium saucepan. Heat gently, stirring occasionally, until sugar dissolves and liquid is clear.

2. Without stirring, cook until mixture turns a golden caramel color. Brush any sugar crystals clinging to the inside of the pot back into the caramel with a brush dipped in cold water. When caramel is golden, stand back, avert face, and add boiling water. Cook just until mixture is smooth, about 30 seconds. Cool to room temperature.

3. Whip cream until light. Slowly beat in half the caramel mixture. Taste. Add more if caramel taste is not strong enough for you. Be careful not to overbeat. (If you end up adding all the caramel, use the whipped cream within an hour; otherwise the cream may start to separate slightly.)

Chocolate Caramel Sauce

YIELD:
Approximately
1-1/2 cups (375 mL)

*T*HIS *is a rich sticky sauce for people who love both caramel and chocolate.*
Serve it over ice cream.

1 cup	granulated sugar	250 mL
3 tbsp	water	50 mL
3/4 cup	whipping cream	175 mL
4 oz	bittersweet or semisweet chocolate, chopped	125 g

1. Place sugar and water in a medium or large heavy saucepan. Cook, stirring constantly, until sugar dissolves.

2. Stop stirring and cook until sugar turns a deep caramel color. Have a bowl of cold water and pastry brush close by. Dip brush in water and brush any sugar crystals from sides of pan back down into liquid sugar mixture. Be careful not to burn caramel. (If you do, start again.) If the sugar crystallizes before turning to caramel, you can add a little more water and continue cooking until crystals melt, or you can begin again.

3. Remove pan from heat and, very carefully (averting your face and standing back), add cream. Continue to cook and stir until sauce is smooth.

4. Add chocolate and stir until melted. Return to heat only if necessary for a minute or two.

5. Serve warm or at room temperature. Sauce will thicken when cold — warm up gently to serve.

A Lighter Side: Use light cream or milk instead of whipping cream.

Dark Chocolate Sauce with Orange

A luscious topping for ice cream or sundaes that can be made ahead in large quantities. If you are not going to use the sauce within a few weeks, freeze it.

YIELD:
Approximately 1-1/3 cups (325 mL)

3/4 cup	granulated sugar	175 mL
1/2 cup	cocoa	125 mL
1/2 cup	milk	125 mL
2 oz	bittersweet or semisweet chocolate, chopped	60 g
1/3 cup	unsalted butter	75 mL
2 tbsp	orange liqueur	25 mL
1 tsp	pure vanilla extract	5 mL

1. In a small or medium saucepan, combine sugar and cocoa. Stir in milk. Whisk in chocolate.

2. Cook on medium heat for 5 minutes, stirring constantly. Remove from heat. Stir in butter, liqueur and vanilla.

A Lighter Side: Substitute water for the milk. Use 2 tbsp (25 mL) butter and omit the bittersweet chocolate.

Grand Marnier Sabayon Sauce

YIELD:
Approximately
3 cups (750 mL)

THIS sauce is light and airy because of the whipped cream, but it can also be served without the cream. It is wonderful with any chocolate dessert.

You can of course use any orange liqueur in this recipe, but there is something extra-special about Grand Marnier.

2 cups	milk	500 mL
2 tbsp	coarsely chopped orange peel	25 mL
6	egg yolks	6
1/3 cup	granulated sugar	75 mL
1/4 cup	Grand Marnier	50 mL
1 cup	whipping cream	250 mL

1. Place milk in a heavy saucepan. Bring just to the boil. Add orange peel. Remove from heat and allow to steep for 15 minutes. Strain.

2. In bowl, beat egg yolks with sugar until pale yellow and thick. Beat in warm milk.

3. Return to saucepan and cook gently, stirring constantly, until slightly thickened. Add Grand Marnier and cook gently about 2 minutes longer.

4. Transfer sauce to bowl and place over a large bowl of ice water. Stir until cool.

5. In separate bowl, whip cream lightly. Fold into cool sauce. Sauce should be creamy but not really thick.

A Lighter Side: Use 2 percent milk and omit the whipping cream.

Crème Fraîche

YIELD:
Approximately
3 cups (750 mL)

C RÈME *fraîche has a very special taste and texture. It is less sweet and dense than whipped cream, but lighter and sweeter than sour cream. It's hard to describe, but not hard to eat. You can serve it beside desserts in a mound (it is marvelous with just about anything) or, if you prefer, thin it with a little whipping cream and whip it so that you can pipe it as a decoration.*

I like two recipes for crème fraîche. Try them both and see which one you prefer. (I make a lot of buttermilk pancakes, so we tend to have buttermilk on hand, but it may be more practical for you to use the sour cream version.)

Remember to make crème fraîche two days before using it, so it will thicken properly. It will keep for one to two weeks in the refrigerator, but you can halve the recipe if you want to make less.

	Version One	
2 cups	whipping cream	500 mL
1 cup	sour cream	250 mL
	Version Two	
3 cups	whipping cream	750 mL
2 tbsp	buttermilk	25 mL

1. In an non-metallic bowl, stir whipping cream with either the sour cream or buttermilk. Cover with plastic wrap.

2. Allow to rest at room temperature for 16 to 24 hours, or until thickened.

3. Refrigerate for 24 hours before using.

Secret Dessert Sauces

YIELD:
Approximately
2 cups (500 mL)

*T*HIS *is more of an idea for a recipe than a recipe itself. And it is a secret. These sauces are so good and so easy that it is embarrassing even to discuss them. But I always tell all!*

If you are in a hurry and want a great sauce for a chocolate cake or soufflé, etc., simply defrost the best ice cream you can find, until it is completely melted. Stir until it is smooth and serve with your dessert. You can add appropriate liqueurs, but most of the time the sauce is great just as is. My favorite is coffee Haagen Dazs over chocolate mousses, soufflés and cakes. I also sometimes use vanilla ice cream with some Grand Marnier — 3 tbsp (50 mL) per 2 cups (500 mL) — for white chocolate desserts or over sliced strawberries. You can use melted sorbets as wonderful fruit sauces, too. Be sure to use the best possible product, however, or the mixture may separate when melted.

Here are a few other possibilities:
   rum or Amaretto with chocolate ice cream;
   orange or Sambucca with coffee ice cream;
   Cognac or orange with vanilla ice cream;
   vanilla ice cream with a little raspberry ice added;
   raspberry ice with raspberry or orange liqueur.

Index

INDEX